Barcode in Back

‖‖‖‖‖‖‖‖‖‖‖‖‖‖‖‖‖‖‖‖‖‖
W9-CZX-902

Career Launcher

Advertising and Public Relations

Career Launcher series

Advertising and Public Relations
Computers and Programming
Education
Energy
Fashion
Film
Finance
Food Services
Health Care Management
Health Care Providers
Hospitality
Internet
Law
Law Enforcement and Public Safety
Manufacturing
Nonprofit Organizations
Performing Arts
Professional Sports Organizations
Real Estate
Recording Industry
Television
Video Games

Career Launcher

Advertising and Public Relations

Stan Tymorek

Ferguson Publishing
An imprint of Infobase Publishing

Career Launcher: **Advertising and Public Relations**

Ferguson
An imprint of Infobase Publishing
132 West 31st Street
New York NY 10001

Library of Congress Cataloging-in-Publication Data

Tymorek, Stan.
  Advertising and public relations / by Stan Tymorek.
    p. cm. — (Career launcher)
  Includes bibliographical references and index.
  ISBN-13: 978-0-8160-7961-2 (hardcover : alk. paper)
  ISBN-10: 0-8160-7961-7 (hardcover : alk. paper)
1. Advertising—Vocationa l guidance. 2. Public relations—Vocational guidance. I. Title.
  HF5828.4.T96 2009
  659.023—dc22

                                                      2009024196

Ferguson books are available at special discounts when purchased in bulk quantities for businesses, associations, institutions, or sales promotions. Please call our Special Sales Department in New York at (212) 967-8800 or (800) 322-8755.

You can find Ferguson on the World Wide Web at http://www.fergpubco.com

Produced by Print Matters, Inc.
Text design by A Good Thing, Inc.
Cover design by Takeshi Takahashi
Cover printed by Art Print Company, Taylor, PA
Book printed and bound by Maple Press, York, PA
Date printed: May 2010

Printed in the United States of America

10 9 8 7 6 5 4 3 2 1

This book is printed on acid-free paper.

Contents

Foreword

Why does advertising matter? Advertising matters for any number of reasons. For one thing, it helps keep our economy moving forward by fueling consumption. This "fueling of consumption" is also what makes advertising controversial, too. Many believe that advertising causes us to buy more "stuff" than we need. That may be true, but I tend to believe we'd buy a lot of that stuff anyway—what advertising does is point us toward certain brands and types of products. We were probably going to buy a car whether we saw advertising or not (what's the alternative, hitchhiking?). But the ads influence our choice of one car over another.

They help us make sense of all the consumer choices before us—and not necessarily in a purely logical way. Ads can help to create an emotional, slightly irrational bond with a brand. The ad—its tone, its style, its subtext—signals to us, "this is the brand for me." This is not such a bad thing, because it brings some clarity to what would otherwise be a chaotic experience of trying to decide among so many similar products and choices. Without advertising, we'd probably have to flip a coin to decide what to spend that coin on.

Advertising also matters because it's a mirror of the culture in which we live. In fact, Marshall McLuhan once described advertisements as "the richest and most faithful daily reflections that any society ever made of its entire range of activities." This means we can learn a lot about ourselves by studying advertising. Advertising is often accused of telling us what to think, manipulating attitudes and behavior—which it sometimes does. But more often, it tries to reflect and reinforce attitudes and behavioral trends that have already begun to take hold in the culture. During boom years, ads tend to show us living the high life; during recessionary times, the ads become more sober and serious. If historians doing research on any particular time period wish to know what people at that time were doing—what they were dreaming, lusting after, worrying about, arguing over—those historians could learn an awful lot just by studying the ads of that period.

For those getting into the business now, it is a very different ad world than it was 10 years ago. Back then, the Internet was still new and most ad creators only needed to know how to do two things—make a TV commercial or create a print ad. (Okay, once in a while they might get stuck doing a radio ad or a billboard too). Today, ad creators must be versatile enough to work in countless media formats—everything from the short Web film to guerrilla advertising that might take the form of something stenciled on the sidewalk. This can be seen as both scary and exhilarating; scary because there's so much to be learned every day, and exhilarating for the same reason.

One thing is certain: There has never been a better time to be young in advertising. In a way, young people rule advertising now to an extent they never have before. The business is being completely reinvented with an emphasis on new media and fresh approaches. If you're new to the ad business, this is good news for you. Change is your friend, while it is the enemy of old, grizzled veterans. You're not weighed down by the old conventions; you're freer to experiment and make up the rules as you go. That said, you should probably make sure you have a very good understanding and knowledge of the old rules before setting out to break them.

Even as everything in the business seems to be changing, there are certain constants. The value of a good story has not diminished. The ability to tell a story well—whether it is humorous or heartbreaking—is still what separates the heroes from the hacks. A few other things that will never go out of style: Empathy. Originality. And maybe most important, resiliency. Advertising is a business where ideas get killed every day. Some of those will be your ideas. You will love them and swear they are brilliant. They will get killed anyway, sometimes with good reason and sometimes not. It doesn't matter—all that matters is that you sit down and come up with another idea that is even better. The people who can do that tend to do well in advertising.

Here's another tip: Don't spend too much time trying to emulate or imitate other people's award-winning ads. What will tend to make you stand out as an ad person is your unique view of the world, your own slightly skewed perspective. Great ad people do an interesting balancing act: They always tell the story of a brand, but at the same time they're somehow telling a little bit of their own stories as people, too.

Don't be afraid of making ads that are too weird or idiosyncratic. Those are the best kinds of ads, because they reveal the quirkiness of the individual. I refer to strange ads as "oddvertising." And it's the kind of advertising I most enjoy watching, because you never know what's going to happen next.

The world is at a place now where we have to do a lot of reinventing and rebuilding; we need to clean up a lot of the messes that have been created in recent years. I believe advertising can be part of the rebuilding process (just as it was part of creating the mess). It can spread optimistic messages. It can tell inspiring stories that are going on all around us. It can rally public support behind worthy efforts and programs and innovations. But it can only do this if the ads are created with a sense of honesty, authenticity, and imagination. We don't need more propaganda; we don't need a lot of empty, insincere hype. We need people who can communicate the dreams and aspirations of entrepreneurs, of product designers, of the people who make and build. At its best, this is what advertising does—it tells us the story behind a company or a brand or a group of people who make things. It puts a human face on commerce.

—Warren Berger
JOURNALIST AND AUTHOR

Acknowledgments

The author wishes to thank: At Print Matters, Richard Rothschild for the assignment and David Andrews for his encouragement, astute editing, and suggestions; Warren Berger for his Foreword's refreshing perspective on the industry; and Barry Biederman, Jon Steel, and Penelope Trunk for their insightful answers to my interview questions.

Since the advertising and public relations industries are being transformed by the Internet, it makes sense that two online resources were especially useful: the Web site http://www.ihaveanidea.com, and Penelope Trunk's Brazen Careerist blog (http://blog.penelopetrunk.com). Trunk's advice for people in any industry, at any stage of their careers is both practical and inspiring.

As always, Jan Tymorek was an essential, creative partner.

Introduction

One thing you probably already know about advertising is that it makes the most of imagination. In the world of advertising raisins dance, babies talk about their investment strategy, and dough springs to life. So it seems appropriate to begin a book about advertising and public relations with a little fantasy.

Let's say you're an art director with a few years in the business who has just started working at a new agency job. One day in the break room you sit down next to two account planners who are discussing Jon Steel, who in 1996 wrote one of the seminal books on getting customers' input while creating ads. "I wonder what Steel would think of planners reading blogs to get customer opinions," one planner says to the other. "Oh, I read an interview with him and he cautioned that blogs are no substitute for talking directly with customers," you say. "But speaking of blogs, I also read that a career advisor says they're essential for professional growth."

The situation may be fictitious, but the opinions the art director referred to can be found right here in *Career Launcher: Advertising and Public Relations*. This concise book will provide you with in-depth, insider information about the industries that could have taken you years to acquire on your own. You'll appreciate that convenience, because one thing you'll find out about the fast-paced ad world is you have very little spare time.

The following are some of the main areas that this book addresses, introduced with one of advertising's favorite devices: the headline.

Like a Good Ad Campaign, This Book Has Goals

Your clients want to know what kind of results they will get from your agency's work. You should expect the same from this book, so here are its intentions.

You'll learn enough about the history of advertising and public relations to understand how today's practices came to be; become familiar with the classic campaigns and achievements in both industries that are worth emulating (and imitating); get to know the legendary leaders from the past and why they are revered (and to be able to chime in at lunch when some veteran starts quoting one of the greats); see the "big picture" of your industry to understand where you fit in now and where you'd like to go; appreciate the jobs of colleagues in other departments and know whom to turn to with specific questions; make significant contributions to your company and plan your career strategically; learn the lingo of your profession (so staffers in different disciplines can talk to each other); and find other good sources of information (with books, remember to check out their goals).

That's what this book sets out to do. Ultimately, how well it does its job will be determined by how much it helps you do yours.

Find Facts Fast!

This book is designed to make the information bite-sized and easy to find. Of course you can read it linearly from cover to cover (as you did in college, at least with the short books), but you can also scan the text and go directly to the sections you're interested in (that should make many art directors happy).

Probably the best approach is to go through the whole book so you know all the topics that are covered. Then when you have a question about a certain aspect of the business, you can go right to the relevant section.

You'll also find a good number of boxed features sprinkled throughout the book. They let you spot fast facts, best practices, and other key information at a glance.

Most importantly, this book offers you practical information and advice. So the best way to use it is to apply what you learn to your job.

Advertising and Public Relations: Same Family, Unique Functions

Both advertising and public relations make up one book because they have a lot in common. Even the Bureau of Labor Statistics' official classification of industries puts both of them in the same category. And as you may discover in your career, some people in other professions don't know there is a difference between the two industries.

Obviously there are many differences between selling with paid-for advertising and the "softer" promoting of goods and services that is PR's specialty. As you'll learn in the "Industry History" chapter, public relations, broadly defined, goes back much further than advertising, to the earliest communications in society. Then each profession developed its own specialties when public relations and advertising agencies were founded around the same time, in the late 19th and early 20th centuries. So although I tell the stories of these industries in one narrative, I will also highlight the events that have been most important in each industry, like the Creative Revolution of the 1960s in advertising and the public relations practitioners' response following the 9/11 attacks.

What Good Is History When Advertising's about "The Next Great Thing?"

It's not that those who don't learn about bad campaigns of the past are doomed to repeat them. Instead, knowing about the history of advertising will help you understand where some of today's practices came from. In addition, there are certain themes that have recurred in the industry during the last century and up until today, like attempts to view advertising as a science that can be measured and the conflicting view that unscientific creativity drives the business. And even in this era when so much new technology is changing the industry every year, at its center is still how to sell products and services to people, whose fundamental needs, emotions, and motivations by definition remain pretty much the same.

So it really is worthwhile to learn more about the history of advertising than you would by just watching *Mad Men*.

Public Relations and Advertising Could Both Use Some Good PR

When you tell people what your profession is, they probably don't start looking for a halo over year head. Both advertising and PR have gotten a bum rap over the years. One of the sources of that is a man who figures prominently in the history of both industries: P. T. Barnum, of Barnum & Bailey Circus fame. Barnum's idea of copywriting to promote some of his entertainment acts included sending letters about them to newspapers anonymously or under someone else's name. In his book *Personalities and Products: A Historical Perspective on Advertising in America*, Edd Applegate describes how in 1841 Barnum "improvised" to attract patrons to his museum of curiosities:

Barnum instructed a man to place bricks on the corners of several
streets. Barnum then instructed him to carry at least one brick
to each corner and exchange it for another. The man was not to
comment to anyone. On the hour, he was to go to the museum
and present a ticket, then enter. Within the first hour, approximately 500 men and women stood and watched trying to solve the
mystery. When the man went to the museum, they followed and
purchased tickets, hoping to learn the answer inside.

Of course they never did. Your textbook on contemporary marketing practices probably didn't include that practice.

A century later, the portrayal of advertising didn't make it seem
much better. In the 1946 novel *The Hucksters*, written by a former
copywriter, a client tells his adman, "Two things make good advertising. One, a good simple idea. Two, repetition. And by repetition,
by God, I mean until the public is so irritated with it, they'll buy
your brand because they bloody well can't forget it."

Today, in copywriter Luke Sullivan's book *Hey, Whipple, Squeeze
This* (a title that expresses his irritation with the grocer in an old commercial who asked shoppers, "Please don't squeeze the Charmin"),
Sullivan laments about his own industry's showing in the annual
Gallup poll of most- and least-trusted professions: "...every year,
advertising practitioners trade last or second-to-last place with used
car salesmen and members of Congress."

Public relations practitioners don't fare much better in the public's eye. PR has become almost synonymous with the S-word: spin,
the practice of twisting the truth. Stuart Ewen even titled his 1998
book *PR! A Social History of Spin*.

What do these less-than-glowing opinions of the industry mean?
For one thing, a cynical public who has seen lots of outdated tricks is
much more savvy. That makes your job harder and should motivate
you to do more intelligent work.

In fact, Sullivan quotes Norman Berry, a former creative director
at Ogilvy & Mather, on setting higher standards for advertising: "Of
course, advertising must sell. By any definition it is lousy advertising
if it doesn't. But if sales are achieved with work that is in bad taste
or is intellectual garbage, it shouldn't be applauded no matter how
much it sells."

In a selection of quotes at the beginning of his public relations
book, Ewen acknowledges the undeniable importance of public

opinion, which should give PR practitioners both a feeling a pride and a sense of responsibility. Here's one of them: "Public sentiment is everything. With public sentiment nothing can fail; without it nothing can succeed. He who molds public sentiment goes deeper than he who enacts statutes or decisions possible or impossible to execute."

This quote is from a man who is not known as a spinmeister: Abraham Lincoln.

Directions to a Corner Office (Can MapQuest Do This?)

You're probably happy to have gotten your foot in the door of the profession you chose. And rightly so. But chances are that before long you'll be listening for opportunities knocking, or eyeing the empty seats of coworkers formerly in positions that interest you. Statistics show that workers of ages 18 to 30 stay in a job an average of 18 months. We used to call that "job hopping"; now it's often seen as building your skill set fast.

So this Career Launcher will live up to its name, starting with the timeless way of getting ahead: doing a good job and being recognized for it. You'll also find advice on career planning specific to advertising, like the teachings at a new "boot camp" for novices in the industry who want to move up the ladder, and the personal experiences of a group of young advertising practitioners whose careers have already started to take off. There's even a new MBA program just for creatives, the Berlin School of Creative Leadership, where they can learn to manage global enterprises directly from some of the industry's gurus.

In public relations, there's a formal way to demonstrate what you've learned about the business: certification by the Public Relations Society of America and the Association of Business Communicators. Candidates must have worked in the business for at least five years and must take a written and oral exam. Since there are so many types of PR—from high-tech agencies to corporate communications to sports marketing—the relative merits of specializing in one area and gaining broad experience will be considered.

Since both advertising and public relations can be so demanding that your job can become all consuming, the chapter on career paths will also include tips on striking that elusive balance between your work and your personal life.

Consider the Source

Finding a good mentor is another helpful way of "making it" in these industries. In many respects this book will be mentoring you on your career, so you should know something about me and my professional experience.

Early in my career I worked in the public relations department of an inner-city medical center, eventually becoming director of the department. But for most of my career I was a copywriter and creative director at Lands' End, Inc., where I worked in most of the divisions of this large apparel and home-products company, including its successful Web site. I am now freelancing as a writer and editor.

At the risk of making this section sound too much like my résumé, I want to add that I have also edited two books on poetry and art and have recently finished my first novel. I mention these extracurricular activities to emphasize their value. Both advertising and public relations are fueled by new ideas and creativity. Stimulating outside interests and activities will inspire your thinking on the job, whether or not you're in the official creative department of one of the businesses. As an anonymous poet once wrote, or should have, "All work and no outside interests makes for some very dull campaigns."

Chapter 1

Industry History

In his book *Crystallizing Pubic Opinion* (1923), Edward Bernays, whom many consider to be the father of public relations, wrote: "The three main elements of public relations are practically as old as society: informing people, persuading people, or integrating people with people." Using Bernays's definition, historians of public relations like Scott Cutlip and Don Bates reached far back into history to cite early examples of the industry's practices, including Julius Caesar's reports on his achievements as governor of Gaul, St. Paul's Epistles to the Romans promoting Christianity, and, in the United States, the Founding Fathers' writing of the Federalist papers to win ratification of the Constitution. Following this line of thought, the earliest example of public relations could be Eve's persuading of Adam to eat the forbidden apple. And if Satan had paid Eve to sing the fruit's praises, that could be considered the first advertisement.

But for the purposes of a twenty-first-century career in advertising or public relations, it is more relevant to begin the history of both these professions with someone mentioned in the Introduction, a nineteenth-century American who cut a figure large enough to encompass both advertising and public relations. Ladies and gentlemen, step right up and meet the one, the only P. T. Barnum!

As mentioned in the Introduction, many would say that Barnum did so much damage to the image of promotion that it's probably good there was only one of him. As Edd Applegate points out in *Personalities and Products: A Historical Perspective on Advertising in America*, he became the very embodiment of the term huckster through his imaginative stunts. He piqued public interest in a woman claiming to be the 161-year-old former slave of George Washington by daring the curious to see if she was for real, advertising her as "a humbug, a deception cleverly made of India rubber, whalebone, and hidden springs." (Barnum himself was deceived, as he learned after her death she was only 80 years old.) To make the most of opera star Jenny Lind's first tour of America, his "pre-publicity" included a trumped-up account of Lind's charitable performances and a letter to the *New York Daily Tribune*, written in the name of her composer, marveling how of late her "voice has acquired—if that were possible—even additional powers and effect...." Even dead animals were fair game for his wild campaigns, as when Jumbo, his famous elephant circus star, was killed in a train accident that also injured a smaller elephant. Barnum told the press that Jumbo had protected the smaller animal, a bit of heart-tugging hype that did wonders for attendance at exhibitions of the stuffed Jumbo.

Applegate gives credit where credit's due, pointing out that Barnum initiated advertising techniques that are still practiced, though more honestly, today: keeping a name or business before the public, inventing novel ways to produce conversation about a promotion, capitalizing on every opportunity to garner the attention of the media, and providing more real value than one's competition—more than the customer expected.

In *They Laughed When I Sat Down: An Informal History of Advertising in Words and Pictures*, Frank Rowsome Jr. writes that Barnum changed advertising, which was previously "a series of announcements, a process but not a progression," with the principle "that any promotion should have a carefully timed sequence, leading up to a crescendo of interlocked advertising and publicity."

Robber Barons: Rich Men with Poor PR

Their very nickname encapsulates what today is called an "image problem." At the turn of the nineteenth century, the robber barons were too busy exploiting the abundant resources of the United States to worry about what ordinary citizens thought of them. Among them was Henry Clay Frick, who in 1892 called upon the Pennsylvania State Militia to break a strike by the labor union in the Carnegie-Frick Steel Companies plant in Homestead, Pennsylvania; and William Henry Vanderbilt, who in 1883, when questioned by a

Fast Facts

Top Campaigns of the 20th Century

Volkswagen, "Think small," Doyle Dane Bernbach, 1959

Coca-Cola, "The pause that refreshes," D'Arcy Co., 1929

Marlboro, The Marlboro Man, Leo Burnett Co., 1955

Nike, "Just do it," Wieden & Kennedy, 1988

McDonald's, "You deserve a break today," Needham, Harper & Steers, 1971

DeBeers, "A diamond is forever," N.W. Ayer & Son, 1948

Absolut Vodka, The Absolut Bottle, TBWA, 1981

Miller Lite beer, "Tastes great, less filling," McCann-Erickson Worldwide, 1974

Clairol, "Does she...or doesn't she?" Foote, Cone & Belding, 1957

Avis, "We try harder," Doyle Dane Bernbach, 1963

Source: "The Advertising Century," AdAge.com

reporter about the discontinuance of a fast mail train popular with the public, declared: "The public be damned!"

Yet at the same time the public was becoming too much of a force to be so summarily dismissed. In *PR! A Social History of Spin*, Stuart Ewen describes how the burgeoning newspapers, magazines and telegraph of the early twentieth century "were being seen as cognitive connecting points joining an extensive highway of perception." The media were replacing the image of the unruly crowd, whom business leaders both belittled and feared, with that of a public who "might—if strategically approached—be reasoned with" and who "seemed more receptive to ideas, to rationalization, to the allure of factual proof."

Out of this new media era came a newspaper reporter with allegiances to big business, Ivy L. Lee. In 1903, Lee started one of the first public relations agencies and established practices that are still in use today. According to Ewen, Lee laid out the new century's scenario to a group of railroad executives in 1916, when he said they "are not running a business, but running a business of which the public itself is taking complete supervision." The only option for them and the leaders of all industries, he warned, was to make use of the popular media to promote their own interests. His public relations agency would be happy to show them how.

First the captains of industry had to abandon their old habit of corporate secrecy and openly give the public the facts. Fostering a scientific image, Lee referred to himself as a "physician for corporate bodies" while Gerard Stanley Lee, his brother-in-law and fellow PR pioneer, preferred to be known as a "news engineer." Their initial clients called on them in times of crisis, as when the Anthracite Coal Operators' Committee of Seven was threatened with a strike in 1906. "Newspaper editors were flattered by the initial display of openness," Ewen writes, "and the coal operators received better treatment in the press."

A better-known example of Lee's crisis control is his counsel for the Rockefeller family after the violent strike on their Ludlow, Colorado, mine resulted in the deaths of miners, women, and children. To tell the company's side of the story, he flooded the country's opinion leaders with "fact-filled broadsides" about the crisis. However, it was later shown that many of these "facts" were not true. In an investigation of the Ludlow incident, conducted by the Federal Industries Relations Committee, Lee stated that he made no effort to confirm the information given to him by the Rockefellers. No wonder early skeptics of public relations took to calling Ivy Lee "Poison Ivy." Lee himself supplied a name for the PR industry: He dubbed the relation between public interest and corporate policy a "two-way street"—an ideal never realized in his career.

The Origins of Ad Agencies

Advertising in America began in the colonial days with newspapers printing concise notices in a separate section of the paper, similar to today's classified ads. The best-known of these early newspaper ad men was Benjamin Franklin, publisher of the *Pennsylvania Gazette*, in Philadelphia. As recorded in *Personalities and Products: A Historical Perspective on Advertising in America*, by Edd Applegate, a 1735 issue contained this ad: "VERY good COFFEE sold by the Printer hereof."

It wasn't until 1868 that the first full-blown ad agency was founded: N. W. Ayer & Son, in Philadelphia. At that time ad agencies represented advertisers but were paid by publishers. This arrangement did not make sense to Frances Wayland Ayer (the son). So he changed his agency to be the representative of his client advertisers, and more significantly, to let them know the cost of ad space and charge a flat commission of 12.5 percent (a figure that later rose to 15 percent and became the industry standard for many years). Another Ayer innovation that Applegate cites is a market survey of grain production by state to attract a threshing machine company, the first survey of its kind.

A new service that Ayer added for his clients was copywriting, which had begun to be recognized as key to an ad's effectiveness. The foremost copywriter of this era did not work for Ayer or any other agency; he was an independent named John E. Powers. As Randall Rothenberg wrote in the 1999 article "The Advertising Century" in *Advertising Age,* Powers was known as the "father of modern creative advertising." He claimed, "Fine writing is offensive," suggesting instead "simple, short, lively, cogent reason-why copy that was, significantly, truthful." One of his ads for the Wanamaker department store, in Philadelphia, began, "We have a lot of rotten gossamers and things we want to get rid of." According to "The Advertising Century," the ad "sold out the lot in hours."

Advertising Worked—But How?

That department store's founder, John Wanamaker, is credited with one of the most memorable quotes in advertising history. Well aware of the power of advertising as evidenced by the Powers ad, he also wondered, "I know I waste half the money I spend on advertising. The problem is, I don't know which half." The insecurity of not being able to pinpoint just how their ads produced results for their clients led agencies to "giving away more and more functions for their commissions," wrote Randall Rothenberg in his history for *Advertising Age,* also called "The Advertising Century." To support this view of the industry, Rothenberg quotes advertising legend Albert Laskar, who became the head of the Lord & Thomas agency in the first part of the twentieth century: "'My idea of this business,' he said many years later, 'was to render service and make money.'"

Yet during his career Laskar became very good at judging the effectiveness of one of these services, "sloganeering," or copywriting, and at hiring top writers. In *Personalities and Products,* Applegate recounts how the copywriter John E. Kennedy convinced Laskar that advertising was "salesmanship in print" and that "consumers needed a reason to buy something." Another very successful Lord & Thomas writer, Claude C. Hopkins, got selling ideas from seeing how products were manufactured, according to Applegate, and conducted tests to see which headlines and body-copy sentences were most effective. Taking a cue from Hopkins when he landed the Sunkist Growers, Inc. account, Laskar found out that California citrus growers produced so many oranges that they cut down orange trees to limit the supply. Laskar thought this was wasteful and saw an opportunity to increase sales. So he directed the creation of ads promoting the drinking of orange juice as well as the eating of the fruit. They worked: The ads increased consumption of oranges and saved trees.

Throughout the history of advertising, smart ad men and women would continue to try to answer Wanamaker's question about how to measure the effectiveness of advertising.

The Birth of the Brand

In 1927, competition between the two major automobile companies resulted in a marketing concept that soon became integral to almost all industries, according to Rothenberg's "The Advertising Century." Two decades earlier Henry Ford began mass production to make the Model T's price affordable for all middle-class Americans, and by 1927 he had successfully saturated the auto market. So Alfred Sloan of General Motors realized that for his company to grow, he had to change consumers' view of the automobile from a basic mode of transportation to a status symbol for which consumers would "continually upgrade." Thus America entered the era of "planned obsolescence through cosmetic changes" and upwardly mobile consumers demonstrating Thorstein Veblen's concept of "conspicuous consumption."

GM's surpassing of Ford in sales through this approach raised a basic question for the U. S. economy: If status perceptions and cosmetic changes were more important to sales than actual product improvements and lower costs, then marketing the long-term brand instead of short-lived products might be more productive. Support for this theory of the brand came from a young Harvard graduate named Neil McElroy, who joined Procter & Gamble Co. in 1931. McElroy convinced upper management that each brand in the company was a business to be managed by a dedicated team, Rothenberg states. All marketing efforts were to be focused on driving that brand to the top position in its category and to establishing its lasting identity in the public's perception.

Edward L. Bernays: Father of "Spin"?

Just when advertising was beginning to focus more on consumers' perceptions than products' specifics, public relations came under the spell of one of the all-time experts on public opinion. Besides *Crystallizing Public Opinion* Edward L. Bernays was also the author of the other influential PR works *Propaganda* (1928) and "The Engineering of Consent" (1947). In the 1920s he initiated the joining of corporate sales and social issues with the "Torches of Freedom event," organizing women's rights advocates in New York City to march while holding up Lucky Strike cigarettes (his client); and he pulled off the first "global media event" with a worldwide celebration commemorating the 50th anniversary of the electric light bulb (sponsored by General Electric).

Though Bernays's theories may be too close to what we now call "spin" for contemporary PR practitioners to endorse wholeheartedly, they have had a lasting influence on the industry. In *PR! The Social*

Everyone
Knows

Top Slogans of the 20th Century

"Just do it" (Nike)

"The pause that refreshes" (Coca-Cola)

"Tastes great, less filling" (Miller Lite)

"We try harder" (Avis)

"Good to the last drop" (Maxwell House)

"Breakfast of champions" (Wheaties)

"Does she ... or doesn't she?" (Clairol)

"When it rains it pours" (Morton Salt)

"Where's the beef?" (Wendy's)

Source: "The Advertising Century," AdAge.com

History of Spin, Stuart Ewen outlines Bernays's steps that a public relations specialist should take to "become the creator of circumstance." The specialist must first study the media through which the majority of people form their "picture" of the world. Most people, according to Bernays, "like to hear new things in accustomed ways."

"Second," Ewen explains, "those interested in fashioning public opinion must be sociologically and anthropologically informed; they must be meticulous students of the social structure and of the cultural routines through which opinions take hold on an interpersonal level." Above all, Bernays believed, the PR specialist must closely study the public psyche. "If we understand the mechanism and motives of the group mind," he asked rhetorically, "is it not possible to control and regiment the masses according to our will without their knowing it?"

Bernays's talk of "control," "regiment," and "will" smacks too much of propaganda (again, the name of one of his books) for today's public relations professionals and for the public. The next generation of industry leaders would come to respect fact and reason considerably more than their often overbearing forefather.

Research Goes to Market

While public relations was theorizing about mass psychology, forward thinkers in advertising were applying scientific research to consumer behavior. This new development began in 1921, when the J. Walter Thompson agency hired behavioral psychologist John Watson to help the agency plumb consumers' minds. Then research shifted into high gear when a professor of advertising (yes, the industry was legitimized by academia by this time) and journalist named George Gallup joined the Young & Rubicam agency in 1932. As Mark Tungate writes in *Adland: A Global History of Advertising*, Gallup had already made his name in the ad world through his research on magazine readership, especially his results showing what types of magazine ads were most effective. "He discovered that while the largest percentage of ads focused on the economy and efficiency of products, those that pushed the right buttons with readers concerned quality, vanity and sex-appeal," according to Tungate.

So here was a case of using science in advertising only to discover the importance of the nonscientific elements of the business. But founder Raymond Rubicam was sold on Gallup, for although his agency had a reputation for creativity, as Tungate writes, "Ideas based on facts became his mantra." Gallup's research department eventually grew to 400 people around the country asking questions for Y&R, and other agencies added market research to their toolbox. Eventually, in 1958, the researcher went out on his own to establish the Gallup Organization, and the questioner of households became a household name.

Radio Days

When the BBC launched on "the wireless" in the United Kingdom in 1922, it was ad-free. But in the United States, as Tungate's *Adland* points out, the new medium sang a different tune. Here advertisers both sponsored and produced most of the radio shows. "Dark mutterings about advertising 'intruding on the family circle' were drowned out by the sound of the Lucky Strike Dance Orchestra," Tungate writes.

Beginning with National Carbons Company's first sponsorship of a regular series of broadcasts, the *Eveready Hour*, in 1923, American radio audiences were entertained with a whole lineup of product-name series, according to *Advertising Age*'s "The Advertising Century" timeline. Some agencies found their fortunes on the radio waves, like Benton & Bowles, whose variety show *The Maxwell House Showboat* "spurred an 85 percent rise in sales in a single year," as Tungate notes in *Adland*. Frank Hummert, an adman with the Blackett & Sample agency, had the distinction of creating the "soap opera," cliff-hanging serials often sponsored by detergents. Hummert's longest-running soap opera was, according to Tungate, *Ma Perkins*: It ran for 37 years.

The revolutionary electronic media reached a milestone in 1938, *Advertising Age* reports: Radio surpassed magazines as a source of ad revenue.

Postwar Prosperity Prompts Battle of the Agencies

Among the reasons for the advertising industry's rapid growth after World War II was the new medium of television. But the dramatic convergence of all the contributing causes seems to have been scripted for the Hollywood movies.

As Rothenberg points out in "The Advertising Century," the postwar economic expansion created a new prosperity in the country. The widespread use of automobiles led to a uniform landscape of motels, fast-food restaurants, and chain stores—an environment in which "a powerful brand could have national, even multinational reach." The auto and its highways also made suburbia appealing, allowing the middle class to hold down well-paying jobs near the city while having houses, yards, and children. When televisions were plugged into these houses, it was like a bolt of electricity hit the ad business. Rothenberg cites one example: "Hazel Bishop lipstick sales skyrocketed from $50,000 a year in 1950 to $4.5 million two years later thanks to TV advertising."

With the stakes now higher than ever, competition between different advertising theories intensified. In the latest installment of the creativity versus pragmatism debate, according to Rothenberg, David Ogilvy of Ogilvy & Mather claimed it was "brand personality" and not a "trivial product difference" that sold products. In the other corner, Rosser Reeves defined and stood behind the "Unique Selling Proposition," the one claim that differentiated a product from its competition. Rothenberg cites Martin Mayer's comment on this face-off in his chronicle *Madison Ave. U.S.A.*: "Each shakes his head over the way the other wastes his clients' money."

Advertisers as "Hidden Persuaders"

One of the most controversial books ever written about advertising was Vance Packard's *The Hidden Persuaders*, published in 1957. Curiously, the best-selling book is commonly linked to the maligned use of subliminal messages—words or images that are embedded in another medium and unrecognized by the conscious mind, yet are able to affect the subconscious mind—but this concept is just touched on in Packard's book.

In *Adland* Tungate describes the real focus of *The Hidden Persuaders*: "'Large-scale efforts are being made,' Packard warned, 'to channel our thinking habits, our purchasing decisions, and our thought processes . . . .' He claimed that scientists were furnishing advertising agencies with 'awesome tools,' with the result that 'many of us are being influenced and manipulated, far more than we realize, in the patterns of our everyday lives.'" One such scientist, according to Tungate, was Ernest Dichter, who in the late 1930s introduced "depth interviews" to uncover consumers' attitudes toward products. By the 1950s several major agencies were using this kind of motivational research.

In an article from Salon.com published shortly after Packard's death in 1996, "The Hidden Persuaders," David Futrelle chides the writers of media obituaries who overemphasized the late author's work on subliminal advertising. "In fact," Futrelle writes, "Packard devoted minimal attention to the subject—the word 'subliminal' doesn't even appear in the book—and treated reports of 'subthreshold effects' with some skepticism." It seems that while Packard was writing *The Hidden Persuaders*, market researcher James Vicary claimed in his testimony that quickly flashing messages on a movie screen, in Fort Lee, New Jersey, had influenced people to purchase more food and drinks. Even though Vicary later admitted he had falsified his results, the combination of this alarming claim and Packard's well-researched book led the National Association of Broadcasters to ban subliminal advertising in 1958.

A Little Car Ignites a Big Revolution

Given the great variety of forceful personalities, competing theories, and creative approaches in advertising's history, it is quite remarkable that so much attention is still given to one man, one product, and one word. The ad in which all three came together was the opening salvo in the "Creative Revolution"—the shot heard 'round the business world.

In 1959, Bill Bernbach, the head of creative at the Doyle Dane Bernbach agency, began working on an ad campaign for Volkswagen. In an era accustomed to the "exaggerated iridescence of Detroit's advertising," as Randall Rothenberg has called it, Bernbach and his art director showed a VW bug in stark black and white, and beneath it the spare headline "Lemon." The body copy went on to explain that this perfectly fine-looking car had been rejected by one of the car company's demanding inspectors, who had noticed a mere blemish on the glove compartment's chrome strip.

If this innovative VW ad is the example advertising writers love to cite, Bernbach is the adman they love to quote. And for good reason: As Luke Sullivan remarks in *Hey Whipple, Squeeze This*, Bernbach respected the intelligence of both ad creators and consumers, founding his agency "on the then radical notion that customers aren't nitwits who need to be fooled or lectured or hammered into listening to a client's sales message." Later in his book Sullivan includes a quote from Bernbach that could stand for the credo of the Creative Revolution:

However much we would like advertising to be a science—because life would be simpler that way—the fact is that it is not. It is a subtle, ever-changing art, defying formularization, flowering on freshness and withering on imitation; what was effective one day, for that very reason, will not be effective the next, because it has lost the maximum impact of originality.

Rothenberg's quotes from the revolution's leader are pithier: "'Advertising,' he wrote, 'is fundamentally persuasion.' And persuasion is 'an art.'" Regarding the goal of creating provocative, imaginative ads, Bernbach said, "If breaking every rule in the world is going to achieve that, I want those rules broken."

The times were ripe for the Creative Revolution, as the 1960s counterculture was questioning the status quo in almost every segment of society. Creative types who were earning their living in agencies instead of the arts still strove for freedom of expression. Just as Doyle Dane Bernbach (DDB) conceived a campaign for Levy's rye bread featuring members of various ethnic groups and the line "You don't have to be Jewish to love Levy's," you didn't have to be from DDB to be creative. As Rothenberg notes, when art director Steve Frankfort became in charge of creative at Young & Rubicam, the agency produced memorable ads for clients as diverse as Johnson & Johnson and the National Urban League. Account executive Carl Ally started his own agency, Mark Tungate notes in *Adland*, and set the tone with a sign in his office that said, "Comfort the afflicted; afflict the comfortable." His agency famously touted Volvo's durability with the line, "Drive it like you hate it." Meanwhile in Chicago, even during the pre-revolutionary 1950s, the Leo Burnett agency was giving birth to such industry icons as Tony the Tiger, the Jolly Green Giant, and the Pillsbury Doughboy. (Tungate quotes Burnett on his characters: "None of us can underestimate the glacier-like power of friendly familiarity.")

Public Relations in the 1960s: "The Customer Is King"

This decade was also a time of growth in the public relations industry. For along with the 1960s countercultural creativity came a new activism among many groups, including consumers. Groups were formed to protect citizens from unsafe products, dangerous working conditions, and other breaches of "the expanding social contract," according to a paper by Don Bates called "Mini-Me History: Public Relations from the Dawn of Civilization." Two popular targets of consumer activities were corporations, which then instituted customers' "Bills of Rights" and other concessions to keep customers satisfied, and universities, many of which were epicenters of countercultural activity among both faculty and students. Both institutions suddenly became more accountable to their "publics" and needed to forge good relations with them.

"The New Gods Wore Suits and Came Bearing Calculators"

That's how Luke Sullivan sums up the end of the Creative Revolution and the beginning of new era in *Hey Whipple, Squeeze This*. In "The Advertising Century" Richard Rothenberg is more analytical, citing such reasons for the transition in the next decade as "the shrinkage of ad budgets during the 1970s recession, the public stock offerings of rebel shops like PKL (Papert Koenig Lois), and the procurement of conservative package-goods accounts by several 'swinging agencies.'"

As had happened before in advertising's history, the transition gained momentum due to a theory, in this case one proposed by Professor Theodore Levitt of the Harvard Business School. Rothenberg explains that Professor Levitt thought new communication technologies were "homogenizing markets everywhere," resulting in a "global corporation" that "does and sells the same things in the same single way everywhere." The best example of the global ad agency was "over the pond," as the British say: London's Saatchi & Saatchi.

Brothers from Baghdad Forge an Advertising Empire

Best known for ushering in the era of mega-mergers, the Saatchi brothers' initial interest in advertising stemmed from that creative giant Bill Bernbach. When Charles Saatchi left school at age 17 to go to the States and work as a copywriter, he came under the spell of the pioneering head of DDB. He took this inspiration back to England with him, where he soon produced his own striking ads for the Benson & Bowles agency. But it wasn't until 1970, when he teamed up with his younger brother Maurice, fresh out of business school and working for a publishing company, that their last name became the most famous one in the ad business.

The Saatchi & Saatchi notoriety was due in large part to two high-profile ads from about a decade later, according to Tungate in *Adland*. Their work for the Conservative Party included a poster with a photograph of a very long line outside an unemployment office and the headline, "Labour isn't working." A TV commercial for British Airways had the drama of a sci-fi film: a giant shadow passed over British streets, causing residents to look out of their houses. Spectacularly, what looked like the island of Manhattan then landed at Heathrow Airport. The voiceover said, "Every year, British Airways flies more people across the Atlantic than the entire population of Manhattan."

In 1986, Charles Saatchi turned his attention to the United States again; this time he and his brother were announced by *Time* magazine: "The British admen are coming!" In that year the Saatchis had acquired three major U.S. agencies: Backer & Spielvogel, Dancer Fitzgerald, and the largest of the three, Ted Bates Advertising. But this British invasion did not prove to be as popular as the rock 'n roll one two decades earlier. Mark Tungate writes of the brothers' agency: "... the Americans had grown wary of the group, which had waded into the stable, cloistered environment of Madison Avenue and begun dismantling and reconstructing agencies. As a result of these reshuffles, clients occasionally found themselves in bed with their competitor. Some of them leapt right out again."

In 1987, just after a failed attempt to purchase the fourth largest bank in Britain, the Saatchis ran into trouble on another New York City street, Wall Street. The stock market crash in October of that year heralded a reversal of fortune for what was then the biggest advertising agency in the world.

In the States, the Stakes Got Higher

Concurrently in 1986, discussions about an even larger merger were underway. Keith Reinhard, then CEO of Needam Harper Worldwide and another admirer of Bill Bernbach, knew he had to move his agency into the top tier quickly to compete with the small number of merged giants leading the industry. Bernbach had died in 1982, but Reinhard was still very interested in partnering with his DDB agency, Mark Tungate writes. But when he was unable to come to terms with DDB, he started talking to another historic agency—Batten, Barton,

Fast

Facts

Most Influential People In Advertising History

William Bernbach (1911-1982) Doyle Dane Bernbach, New York

Marion Harper Jr. (1916-1989) Interpublic Group of Cos., New York

Leo Burnett (1892-1971) Leo Burnett Co., Chicago

David Ogilvy (1911-1999) Ogilvy & Mather Worldwide, New York

Rosser Reeves (1910-1984) Ted Bates & Co., New York

John Wanamaker (1838-1922) Retailer, Philadelphia

William Paley (1901-1990) CBS, New York

Maurice and Charles Saatchi (1946-) and (1943-) Saatchi & Saatchi, London

Albert Lasker (1880-1952) Lord & Thomas, Chicago

Jay Chiat (1931-2002) Chiat/Day, New York

Source: "The Advertising Century," AdAge.com

Durstin & Osborn (BBDO). Ironically, when Reinhard admitted to BBDO chief Allen Rosenshine that his first choice had been DDB, Rosenshine told him BBDO had approached that same agency, too. Demonstrating that two's a company and three's the largest one in the industry, in late April of the same year the trio formed Omnicom, with billings of $5 billion and more than 10,000 employees.

Yet Omnicom's reign as No. 1 was less than a month, as Saatchi & Saatchi completed their acquisition of Bates in May. But Randall Rothenberg points out that much more important than the seesaw battle to be the biggest was the size of the spoils for the acquired Bates employees: the chairman got $111 million and another 100 staff members became millionaires. This bonanza, Rothenberg claims, shook up the ad industry "more profoundly, perhaps, than any other single event ever."

Why? It seems this extravagant buyout upset the longstanding relationship by which agencies and the corporate marketers who hired them were considered to be "marketing partners," as

INTERVIEW

The Way to the Top in Advertising

Barry Biederman
Former chairman and creative director of Biederman, Kelly and Shaffer

How did you get your start in the business?

It was pure happenstance. Not being able to land the job I wanted in TV news, I went to see a friend of my father's who had a medium-sized advertising agency, hoping that he'd give me a lead to a network news executive. He didn't; instead, having listened to my shameless song and dance, he offered me a job as copywriter. I took him up on it, figuring this would be a temporary hitch. But I caught the bug and never looked back.

How were you able to move up in advertising?

I had several mentors. First, a marvelous guy named Myron Mahler, whose great forte was radio jingles. He was a grandson of the great composer Gustav Mahler; he picked out his tunes on the piano, only in the key of C, but boasted he'd made more money composing than his grandfather did. He initiated me into retail advertising, a superb grounding, where we could read the results of our advertising day by day in what goods were selling. Then there was Emil Frizzard—"Izzy"—a copy chief who took this young kid from a small agency and taught him how to operate within a big-agency structure, and to focus on a single, big idea, and look for executions that would express it cogently.

What were some of the biggest changes during your career?

In creative, the most pronounced trend in my early years was the overwhelming primacy of TV advertising, which had just replaced radio as the medium where big things happened. Over the years TV advertising evolved, as with the move from longer-form commercials—60 seconds was standard, and I remember doing 90 second spots for Xerox—to progressively shorter spots. Then there was the use of humor, especially self-deprecating humor, a brilliant departure at first, but increasingly resulting in pointless, even mindless advertising. The use of celebrities, always a feature of advertising, became more and more widespread.

How about changes on the business side?

I saw account management become a real profession. In my early years too many of the account guys (and they were usually guys) owed their place at the agency to an old fraternity connection, or having been a prep-school buddy of some big client. By the time I hung up my spurs, much of this was gone: Accounts were too big, neither agency nor client could afford empty "suits," and the whole biz was better for it.

In the last half of my career the most significant development was the rise of integrated marketing, coordinating several media in one campaign. Some of us had been doing it throughout our careers. It was one of the reasons I pitched a combined corporate-advertising and PR division to NH&S some 40 years ago. But integrated marketing is where it's all going now, as a consequence of the rise of the Web, the fragmentation of media, and the countless distractions that our audiences are subject to.

You're a veteran of the Creative Revolution of the 1960s. How did that affect your career?
I benefited from it as most copywriters and art directors did. It freed our writing to employ irony, humor, and even a touch of candor. It brought in the idea of writers and art directors working as teams, enriching each other's work: Some of my best headlines were inspired by ADs and some of their best visuals were mine.

What were some the greatest challenges you faced?
Filming commercials for ITT overseas was certainly one. Almost every time we arrived on location—in Germany, Norway, France—we found that the local office had given us inaccurate information. And while the commercials had been cleared well in advance, they had to be rewritten, or whole new commercials devised on the spot, while an expensive film crew stood by waiting to commence shooting.

Another was getting clients to accept that we were being zealous stewards of their dollars. This was especially a problem when dealing with clients with smaller budgets, like the Tri-State Cadillac dealers association, which wanted "factory" quality TV spots, but on a shoe-string budget. We did it, but what a struggle!

What was some of your work that you were most proud of?
Lands' End was a writer's dream account—perhaps the last major national advertising account to be fashioned entirely around long copy. What a delight to be writing about quality products, with a client who respected the copy (rarely, if ever, changing any of it), and to be able to put to use all the writing skills acquired throughout my career. For ITT corporate, I created a series of 60-second mini-documentaries, featuring graphic demonstrations of the company's high-tech innovations, with the theme: "The best ideas are the ideas that help people." At the end of the first year *Ad Age* devoted a page to it, with frames from several of the
(continues on next page)

INTERVIEW

The Way to the Top in Advertising (continued)

commercials, citing the campaign as a breakthrough. The campaign ran for 14 years. My campaign for the Israel Ministry of Tourism ("Come to Israel. Come stay with friends."), built around a series of romantic, 30-second TV playlets, ran in only a handful of major markets. But within a year, it reversed a six-year decline in U.S. tourism to Israel.

What advice would you give to those in advertising today?
Study the masters of the art, even the ones who seem a little out-of-date today. The books of David Ogilvy, Rosser Reeves, and John Caples may have a fine layer of dust on them, but their fundamental ideas are still applicable. Pore over the awards annuals—not to copy anybody's work, but to see how many different ways talented writers and art directors have tackled the same problems. And always read, read, read—everything. You can't ever know too much or where the next idea will come from.

Rothenberg calls them. Suddenly the marketers could not ignore how rich their agency partners were becoming.

Recession Reins in Mega-Mergers

In just a few years the newly formed conglomerate agencies came up against a force even bigger than they were, according to Randall Rothenberg—a worldwide recession. This was just one of the trends that caused a downturn in the whole advertising industry, he reports. Network TV lost 27 percent of its prime-time audience during the 1980s. Clients were starting to use direct marketing and other below-the-line services instead of traditional advertising. By the end of the decade the industry that had recently spawned giants was shrinking, with the average annual growth of 15.7 percent falling to less than 8 percent.

Perhaps the toughest challenge facing advertising as it entered the 1990s was a change in the nature of the products that were coming to market, Rothenberg points out. Instead of a few, recognizable brands in a product category, consumers now had a choice of "a glut of new, undifferentiated products" that beat the old brands on price. The battlefield was set for the white knights of creativity to capture the public's attention, as they had in the 1960s. Although this new era in the 1990s wasn't called a creative revolution, one famous commercial from the time did make use of The Beatles' song "Revolution" to sell athletic shoes.

"Good Enough Is Not Enough"

That motto of Jay Chiat helps explain why he became the leader of the second creative revolution in advertising. He strongly believed that advertising should make use of contemporary art, music, and cinematography not only for aesthetics but to drive sales, according to his obituary in the *New York Times* in 2002. Among his agency's most famous ads was a commercial introducing the Macintosh computer in 1984, shot by filmmaker Ridley Scott in the totalitarian spirit of *1984*, and the Nike ads at the time of the Los Angeles Olympics with Randy Newman singing "I Love L.A."

Chiat exhibited a rare mixture of the rational and the emotional, his creative director told the *Times*. He also stood out among agency heads by contributing to both the creative and the business sides of Chiat/Day, his Los Angeles-based agency. He was known for driving both himself and his staff, prompting those who regularly burned the midnight oil to call their agency "Chiat/Day & Night." Mindful of the infamous mega-mergers in the business, Chiat famously said, "I want to see how big we can get before we get bad."

Not the least of his achievements was proving that an industry leader could thrive far away from New York. During Chiat's heyday of the late 1980s and early 1990s, other geographically diverse agencies came to the fore, such as Fallon McElligott in Minneapolis and Wieden & Kennedy (who utilized "Revolution") in Portland, Oregon.

International Innovator

As the U.S. advertising industry went global in the 1990s, agencies around the world produced creative work that expressed their own cultural viewpoints. The foreign campaign from this era that had the most impact, if not downright shock, was Oliviero Toscani's work for Benetton, in Italy.

A priest kissing a nun, a newborn still attached to the umbilical cord, and a dying AIDS patient with his family were just some of the Benetton ad images that drew both lots of attention and emphatic protests. Against the charges that he was exploiting the lax censorship of the late twentieth century, Toscani countered that he was carrying on a Renaissance tradition, according to Mark Tungate in *Adland*. He compared his relationship with founder Luciano Benetton to the one between Michelangelo and the Pope. Toscani thought that instead of just selling sweaters, Tungate writes, "he considered that Benetton was funding research into alternative approaches to communication." Critics were less high-minded, dubbing the Benetton ads and their imitators "shockvertising."

Yet recounting this history of Benetton's campaigns, beginning with its "United Colors of Benetton" ads highlighting racial diversity, on its 2009 Web site, the company raises an intriguing question: "These were photos that portrayed the 'real' world, fell within the conventions of information, and introduced a new and intriguing question about the fate of advertising: Can marketing and the enormous power of advertising budgets be used to establish a dialogue with consumers that focuses on something other than a company's products? Where was it written that advertising could only portray the absence of conflict and pain?"

The Public Demands Accountability

During the 1980s, the activism directed at social change during the 1960s expanded to address other public concerns like product safety, fair labor practices, and environmental problems such as pollution, deforestation, and global warming. Confronted to explain what they were doing about these problems, the government and corporations relied on PR practitioners to respond to the public's concerns and questions with policy statements and press releases emphasizing their clients' "proactive" solutions. Also during this era, several crises of historic proportions occurred around the globe that would put even the most experienced public relations professionals to the test.

Union Carbide's chemical plant explosion in Bhopal, India, Exxon's oil-tanker spill in Alaska, and Nike's labor practices in Asian plants were among the events that became major news stories with lasting reverberations. Corporate responses to crises like these have become textbook cases that PR students and professionals study to draw lessons that they can apply in future situations, according to

Tony Jaques in his article "Learning from Past Crises—Do Iconic Cases Help or Hinder?", published in *Public Relations Journal* (Winter 2009). Yet Jaques cautions practitioners about "how easy it is to be led to wrong or inappropriate lessons from highly exposed cases." To avoid this pitfall, he proposes the comparative study of crisis cases to determine best practices.

Revolution 2.0

As the new media called the Internet moved full cyber-steam ahead at the end of the 1990s, it became the biggest thing to hit advertising since the Creative Revolution of the 1960s. Now a decade into the new century, the Web's impact seems even bigger than the earlier upheaval. For the Internet ushered in two big trends: the explosion of dot-coms that dramatically increased ad spending in the more established media, and the longer-lasting impact of new kinds of advertising in the digital form that opened a whole new, world for agencies.

Today who remembers the sock puppet mascot for a company called Pets.com, a character that was the darling of the Super Bowl in 2000? Perhaps only advertising historians. But that imaginary spokesperson symbolized the ephemeral dot-com boom. In just the first two months of 1999, according to Mark Tungate in *Adland*, the top 50 Internet advertisers in the United States increased their entire 1998 spend by 280 percent. Outdoor billboards with dot-com logos sprung up profusely in both the United States and the United Kingdom, Tungate reports, with UK billboard advertising rising from 1 million pounds in 1998 to 23 million pounds the following year. However, as a whole the dot-coms did much more to benefit ad agencies than investors or their staffs. Launched by a "vision," scores of sites bit the dust due to the lack of a viable business plan and a bad habit of burning cash.

Given all the new ways of advertising on the Internet that have been introduced in just a few years, it's easy to forget it was originally developed for military, governmental, and educational uses. But as Mark Glaser points out in the MediaShift section of the Web site PBS.org (http://www.PBS.org), the lure of finally being able to track an ad's performance by "click-through rates"—the number of times people clicked on the ad—was too great for advertisers to ignore. However, advertisers soon found out that having an impact on Web users was trickier than they thought it would be, and as

Glaser describes it, they have spent the last decade playing a kind of cat-and-mouse game with consumers.

Despite the benefit of click-through rates, banner ads soon became less effective as people learned to ignore them or installed software to block them. Computer screens became the testing grounds for blinking banners, pop-up ads, and "interstitials"—Web pages that appear before the page that the user intended to view. Advertisers devised new ways to deliver ads, like e-mail, RSS Web feeds used to publish frequently updated Internet content, and ads embedded into online audio and video files. Google very effectively utilized the new pay-per-click system, posting "sponsored links" that appeared next to search results based on keywords that companies had bid on.

As Google and other pay-per-click sites proved the improved efficiency and measurability of this new form of Web advertising, more and more marketers hopped on the e-bandwagon. As explained in "Internet Advertising: The Ultimate Marketing Machine," an Economist.com article, pay-per-click allowed companies to go beyond advertising only their "blockbusters," a small percentage of products in the mass media, to marketing each individual product online, "exploiting the economics of the 'long tail.'"

There are as many Web pages for advertisers as there are keywords that can be typed into a search engine, situations that game players might find themselves in, and so forth. Each one comes with its own context, and almost every context suits some product. If you can track the success of advertising, especially if you can follow sales leads, then marketing ceases to be just a cost-center, with an arbitrary budget allocated to it. Instead, advertising becomes a variable cost of production that measurably results in making more profit.

The advent of the Web also gave rise to a new way of selling known as viral advertising, or strategies that encourage consumers to pass on a selling message to others via the Internet, creating the possibility of an exponential increase in the ad's exposure.

In addition to the popular viral video, these promotions may also include text messages, podcasts, sponsored games, music tracks, and images.

One of the earliest examples of the power of viral advertising was Hotmail's campaign in the late 1990s, according to Lightning Bug, an agency specializing in viral marketing (http://www.lbug.co.uk). By attaching a short promotional message to e-mails sent by Hotmail users, the company managed to recruit 12 million subscribers in just

18 months, at a time when there were far fewer Internet users than there are today. Lightning Bug points out that viral advertising took advantage of new online data such as usage tracking and customer profiles to target "smaller numbers of influential individuals who have the status and connections to spread the message." The resultant savings in media buying spurred the popularity of viral campaigns.

A new advertising media as radically different as the Internet creates not only new tools for advertising, but also new theories of how marketing should use these tools. In "The Advertising Century" Rothenberg asserts that promoting brands is now more crucial than ever, because they are "the only forces powerful enough to draw the audience's eye and income through the chaos of the World Wide Web." For a brand to thrive online, with its interactivity and choices, its advertising should aim to be like any other form of entertainment, or paradoxically for this high-tech medium, "a conversation with a friend."

9/11: Public Relations' "D-Day"

The Internet has also had a significant impact on the public relations industry. The public can now learn about companies through keyword searches, RSS feeds, and e-mail. PR agencies can attract attention to their clients by publishing multimedia content, blogs, and byline articles on Web sites. Campaign effectiveness can more readily be measured with tools like search engine rankings. Some of these new tools came into play on the day that severely tested a number of public relations organizations' responsiveness and crisis-management ability: September 11, 2001.

The terrorist attacks prompted large-scale yet different strategies from the private and public sectors. Merrill Lynch, whose headquarters was right by the twin towers, had to calm the high emotions that trigger investor panic and bank runs; airlines had to communicate immediate improvements in security and passenger safety; retailers like Dunkin' Donuts found themselves taking special precautions for employees of Middle Eastern descent; and the U.S. Defense Department had to respond to 10,000 media hits a day in the aftermath, according to Don Bates's "Mini-Me History: Public Relations from the Dawn of Civilization."

Bates quotes from an article published shortly after 9/11 in the *Public Relations Strategist* (Winter 2002): "The events of Sept. 11 didn't necessarily precipitate a huge change in the way communications leaders do their jobs. Rather, they accelerated the speed of existing trends to decentralize, install better backup technology, and pay more attention to employee concerns. The new irony of crisis communications is we must expect the unexpected—and be ready for it when it happens."

A Brief Chronology

1704: The first newspaper advertisement, an announcement seeking a buyer for an estate in Oyster Bay, Long Island, is published in the *Boston News-Letter*.

1729: Benjamin Franklin begins publishing the *Pennsylvania Gazette* in Philadelphia, which includes pages of "new advertisements."

1843: Volney Palmer opens the first advertising agency in Philadelphia.

1868: With $250, Francis Wayland Ayer opens N.W. Ayer & Son (named after his father) in Philadelphia and implements the first commission system based on "open contracts." His clients include Montgomery Ward and John Wanamaker Department Stores.

1877: James Walter Thompson buys Carlton & Smith from William J. Carlton, paying $500 for the business and $800 for the office furniture. He renames it after himself and moves into general magazine advertising. Later, he invents the position of account executive.

1882: Procter & Gamble Co. begins advertising Ivory soap with an unprecedented budget of $11,000.

1892: *Ladies' Home Journal* bans patent-medicine advertising.

1898: N.W. Ayer helps National Biscuit Co. launch the first prepackaged biscuit, Uneeda, with the slogan "Lest you forget, we say it yet, Uneeda Biscuit." Eventually, the company launches the first million-dollar advertising campaign for Uneeda.

1900: N.W. Ayer establishes a "Business-Getting Department" to plan advertising campaigns based on prospective advertisers' marketing needs. Publicity Bureau of Boston established as first public relations firm.

1904: Industry pioneer Ivy L. Lee becomes a public relations counselor.

1906: Congress passes the Pure Food & Drug Act, forcing product labels to list the active ingredients.

1911: Woodbury Soap breaks its "The skin you love to touch" campaign in the Ladies' Home Journal, marking the first time sex appeal is used in advertising.

1913: Ivy Lee counsels the Rockefellers on response to the Ludlow Massacre.

1914: The Federal Trade Commission Act is passed, and Joseph E. Davies is named the first FTC chairman. Section 5 allows it to issue cease-and-desist orders against dishonest advertising.

1922: AT&T's station WEAF in New York offers 10 minutes of radio time to anyone who would pay $100. The Queensboro Corp., a Long Island real estate firm, buys the first commercials in advertising history.

1923: National Carbon Co.'s "Eveready Hour" is the first regular series of broadcast entertainment and music to be sponsored by an advertiser. Edward L. Bernays publishes *Crystallizing Public Opinion*, the first book on professional pubic relations.

1929: Following the stock market crash, advertising spending plummets from its high of $3.5 billion. It sinks to $1.5 billion by 1933. Bernays stages "Torches of Freedom" march on Fifth Avenue to promote smoking.

1938: Congress passes the 1938 Food, Drug and Cosmetic Act, which gives the Food & Drug Administration regulatory powers over the manufacture and sale of drugs.

1942: The War Advertising Council is organized to help prepare voluntary advertising campaigns for wartime efforts. The council garners $350 million in free public service messages. After the war it is renamed the Advertising Council.

1948: The Public Relations Society of America (PRSA) is founded.

1950: PRSA Code of Ethics is adopted by the industry.

1955: The Marlboro Man campaign debuts, created by the Leo Burnett Co. International Public Relations Association (IPRA) is founded.

1957: Vance Packard's *The Hidden Persuaders*, a potent attack on advertising, is published.

1960: Doyle Dane Bernbach introduces the "creative team" approach of combining a copywriter with an art director to create its "Think small" campaign for Volkswagen.

1965: PRSA Accreditation is established for U.S. agencies. International Association of Business Communicators (IABC) is founded.

1971: The Four A's, ANA and American Advertising Federation launch the National Advertising Review Board to monitor questions of taste and social responsibility in advertising. Congress prohibits broadcast advertising of cigarettes.

1975: The Federal Trade Commission Improvements Act gives the agency clear power to set industry-wide rules and to take knowing violators to federal court to seek civil penalties.

1976: The Supreme Court grants advertising First Amendment protection.

1980: Congress removes the FTC's power to stop "unfair" advertising.

1981: MTV debuts with frenetic video images that change the nature of commercials.

1989: Exxon Valdez oil spill becomes a major corporate PR crisis.

1993: The Internet becomes a reality as 5 million users worldwide get online.

1997: The term "weblog" is coined (later shortened to "blog") to describe a type of Web site usually maintained by an individual with regular entries of commentary commonly displayed in reverse-chronological order. Blogs soon become a significant source of timely opinions, including consumers' evaluations of products and services.

1998: Cigarette makers and state attorneys general draft a $206 billion deal that curbs marketing and settles lawsuits to recover Medicaid costs. Council of Public Relations firms is founded.

1999: "E-commerce" and "dot-com" become the new buzzwords as Internet shopping becomes increasingly popular. Internet advertising breaks the $2 billion mark and heads toward $3 billion.

2000: In April the short-lived Internet bubble bursts, as the free-flowing investment capital of the 1990s dries up and the Nasdaq stock index plunges, causing many dotcoms to go out of business. PRSA Code of Ethics revised as "inspirational guidelines."

2002: PRSA endorses Universal Accreditation as standard for practice.

2003: Spam, unsolicited e-mail, accounts for about half of all e-mails and the bane of servers and inboxes. In December, the Controlling the Assault of Non-Solicited Pornography and Marketing Act of 2003 (CAN-SPAM Act) is enacted, intending to help individuals and businesses control the amount of unsolicited e-mail they receive.

2004: The concept of Web 2.0 is introduced to describe a second generation of Web development and design that facilitates communication, secure information sharing, and collaboration. Web 2.0 has led to Web-based communities, hosted services, and applications such as social-networking sites, video-sharing sites, and blogs.

2007: Mobil advertising via wireless phones becomes the latest innovation in Internet marketing. It is especially effective at reaching younger audiences, and some industry analysts predict this market will be as big as $20 billion by 2011.

Sources: "The Advertising Century," AdAge.com; FactMonster.com; and "Mini-Me" History: Public Relations from the Dawn of Civilization, by Don Bates, 2006

Chapter 2

State of the Industry

In 2006, the year of the Bureau of Labor Statistics' latest figures, there were about 48,000 advertising and public relations "establishments" in the United States. About four out of 10 of these were full-service advertising agencies; about one in six were public relations firms. Many of the largest agencies are international, with a substantial proportion of their revenue coming from abroad. Divisions of companies that produce and place their own advertising or PR messages are not included in these statistics.

The advertising and public relations services industry employed 458,000 wage and salary workers in 2006; an additional 46,800 workers were self-employed.

Although advertising and public relations services firms are located throughout the country, they are concentrated in the largest states and cities. California and New York together account for about one in five firms and more than one in four workers in the industry. Firms vary in size, ranging from one-person shops to international agencies employing thousands of workers. However, 68 percent of all advertising and public relations establishments employ fewer than five people and 9 out of 10 employ fewer than 20.

In 2006, workers in the industry averaged 34.7 hours of work per week, slightly higher than the national average of 33.9. There are fewer opportunities for part-time work than in many other industries; in 2006, 12 percent of advertising and public relations employees worked part time, compared with 15 percent of all workers.

About 74 percent of advertising and public relations employees are 25-to-54 years of age. Very few advertising and public relations services workers are below the age of 20, which reflects the need for postsecondary training or work experience.

Management, business, and financial occupations; professionals and related occupations; and sales and related occupations account for about 63 percent of all jobs in the industries. An additional 27 percent of jobs are in office and administrative support occupations. These employees have varied responsibilities in agencies with only a few workers, and the specific job duties of each worker often are difficult to distinguish. Workers in relatively large firms are more specialized, so the distinctions among occupations are more apparent.

Earnings

In 2006, median annual earnings for key positions in advertising and public relations were, according to the Bureau of Labor Statistics:

Copywriters—$50,650 in advertising.
Art directors—$68,100 in advertising and related services.
Public relations specialists—$47,350.

Median annual earnings in the industries employing the largest numbers of corporate public relations specialists were:

Management companies and enterprises—$52,940.
Business, professional, labor, political, and similar
    organizations—$51,400.
Advertising and related services—$49,980.
Local government—$59,510.
Colleges, universities, and professional schools—$43,330.
Advertising managers—$73,060.
Public relations managers—$82,180.
Web designer (2007 figure)—$47,000 - $71,500.

Outlook

Employment of public relations specialists is expected to grow by 18 percent from 2006 to 2016, faster than average for all occupations. PR specialists with foreign-language skills are expected to be in even

greater demand. Opportunities will increase as PR firms hire con-
tractors to provide services rather than support full-time staff.

Yet landing entry-level public relations jobs will continue to be
competitive, as the number of qualified applicants is expected to
exceed the number of job openings. One reason for this is that many
people are attracted to this profession because of its high profile.
Opportunities may also become limited if legislation, aimed at pro-
tecting public health and safety, further restricts advertising for specific products such as alcoholic beverages and tobacco.

Overall, employment in advertising and public relations is projected to grow 14 percent over the 2006–16 period, compared with
11 percent for all industries combined. New jobs will be created as
the economy expands and generates more products and services
to advertise. But along with these promising indicators comes a
word of caution: Layoffs are common in advertising and public
relations firms when accounts are lost, major clients cut budgets,
or agencies merge.

According to the Bureau of Labor Statistics, the future looks
especially bright for Web designers as a part of "computer systems
design and related services, which is projected to be one of the fast-
est growing industries in the United States economy."

As for managers in these industries, employment is expected to
increase by 12 percent through 2016—about as fast as the average
for all occupations.

Current Trends in Advertising

Global Advertising

Following the Creative Revolution of the 1960s, as discussed in
Chapter 1, Theodore Levitt proposed that twentieth-century communications were "homogenizing" markets around the world where
the same products are sold the same way "everywhere." That was
the beginning of the global ad agency—and just the beginning. The
far-reaching finale of last century's technology, the Internet, spurred
the global economy to evolve very quickly, and advertising has had
to keep up.

In "Y2K84," a presentation posted on the Advertising Educational
Foundation's Web site (http://www.aef.com/on_campus/classroom
/speaker_pres/data/8000), Tim Love, vice chairman, Omnicom
Group Inc., says, "Of the world's 100 largest economic entities today,

Best
Practice

"Owning the Room" at a Presentation

In *Perfect Pitch: The Art of Selling Ideas and Winning New Business*, Jon Steel covers presentation pitfalls, examples of great presenters, and other key concepts. He also shares some helpful tips he has learned as a successful presenter on the often overlooked topic of setting up the room where the pitch team will be trying to sell their ideas to a client.

"The room in which a pitch is delivered should be a physical manifestation of both the agency and its idea."

If the meeting is at a client's conference room, it has to feel "different" on pitch day; if it's at the agency's offices the client must feel that the room is welcoming them in particular.

Covering every wall with all the visual aids that will be used makes the client immediately see "a great volume of work and effort."

The room should be prepared to reflect the key elements of the pitch to tell the creative story "as a wall of hieroglyphics in an Egyptian tomb might tell the story of a Pharaoh's life."

For example: When Steel and his team pitched to Porsche, they filled a wall with pictures young children had drawn of their dream cars, many of which looked like red Porsches. On another wall were pictures adults had drawn of the cars they owned—practical vehicles with "large, economical gas tanks." The pictures helped Steel's team tell their story of how many adults still harbored this childhood dream, but were anxious about what others might think of their flashy car.

In seating arrangements, reduce the distance between the presenter and the audience. Instead of sitting at the ends of a table, presenters should sit along one of the sides as part of the group to encourage more audience participation.

Steel suggests that conference tables be moved to along the sides of the room where they can be used for displays, and that seats without tables be arranged in a semicircle on either side of the projection screen. The audience then sits in chairs arranged in another semicircle that mirrors the team.

To presenters who feel uncomfortable without a table or lectern between them and the audience, Steel says, "they are not soccer players lining up to protect the goal against a firmly struck free kick and should not behave as such. Standing between the agency and client teams creates an implicit connection; it imparts confidence and openness...."

51 are now corporations and 49 are countries." Given the cross-cultural reach of these influential corporations, Love draws the analogy between secondhand smoke and secondhand culture in the global economy:

> Our conversations and messaging are accessible in a far more
> transparent world...Just like my cigar smoke, communications can
> go where we don't intend it to go, get seen and heard by people it
> is not intended for and, sometimes, like smoke, our messages can
> leave a bad smell.

In his EFA presentation, "Borderless Brands" (http://www.aef. com/on_campus/classroom/speaker_pres/data/3007) Marcio Moreira, vice chairman, McCann World Group, posits that we have now reached "Globalization Stage 3." This is a stage of "borderless mindsets" characterized by "insight-driven strategies, concept-driven brands, and interactive messaging." Rounding out this contemporary view of the global economy, Ned Russell, executive vice president, Arnold Worldwide, cites these trends: The consumer now has the upper hand over marketers; media have converged (Russell uses the example of a song composed to sell a cell phone rising to the top of the charts in Korea); and innovative edges do not last long enough to be competitive advantages. His conclusion: Global brands have become more important.

Russell also updates Levitt's description of the world market as a "small and homogenous place" to take into account the ideas of a contemporary professor from the Harvard Business School, Pankaj Ghemewat. Professor Ghemewat has said that global marketers must evaluate the "dimensions of distance" that are still in place in our shrinking world. They are four types of distance: cultural, political, geographic, and economic. To describe this more complex world market, Russell quotes John Menzer, CEO of Walmart, who has said that to succeed in the global economy you have to play "3-D chess on the global, regional and local levels."

Elaborating on the new technology's implications for advertising, Love says that word of mouth has become more important than ever, to the extent that "The first media today is people." He also cites a 2005 study undertaken by Omnicom and Yahoo! on "advertising receptivity" among the "My Media Generation"—13- to 25-year-olds around the world. The study found a striking difference in receptivity to advertising between youth in developing countries and those

Everyone

Knows

Can't Do Better than Cannes

The advertising industry has never lacked for awards recognizing outstanding work; but the most prestigious and coveted awards are handed out at the Cannes Lions International Advertising Festival, which takes place every year in mid-June on the French Riviera, the same site where the annual film festival is held.

While most ad professionals know about the cachet of Cannes— and hope their agencies will send them to the picturesque Mediterranean port every year–the reason why the winning ads are awarded Gold, Silver and Bronze Lions is less obvious. According to Mark Tungate's *Adland*, the name goes back to the early years of the festival in the 1950s, when it alternated between Cannes and Venice. A winged lion is the symbol of Venice's patron saint, St. Mark.

What is the real significance of these Lion awards in the business world and why have major clients also started to attend the Cannes festival? Tungate gets several major players' opinions. Phil Dusenberry, BBDO creative star, says that creative awards are a "report card" but the real prize is "making the cash registers ring." Erik Vevroegen, creative director of TBWA/Paris, and Kevin Roberts, worldwide chief of Saatchi & Saatchi, agree that winning at Cannes raises the reputation of an agency's creative work and helps it attract new talent. And Cilla Snowball, chief of the London agency AMV BBDO, thinks that a Cannes Lion is one way of gauging intangible creativity, "and everyone wants to win one."

is developed ones. The results found "55 percent in Mexico, 54 percent in China, and 68 percent in India agree that advertising is a good way to learn about trends and things to buy," while only "30 percent in France, 32 percent in Germany, and 35 percent in the United States" agree with these views on advertising. And yet the study also found that in all countries surveyed, "young people have taken media programming into their own hands" and "the advent of blogging means that information content doesn't have to come from media conglomerates, allowing for new voices."

Responding to the changing attitudes of both the young and their elders around the world, Moreira declares that for the global agency "there are not geographical or economic borders, just emotional borders." That's why in today's marketplace, advertisers should not focus on countries but global "like-minded constituencies." One result of this new playing field is that instead of studying customers' past behaviors, Moreira says, agencies must discover how customers will feel and act next, and then use all their creative resources to be appealing in that future scenario. Moreira does not say this will be easy; in fact, he quotes Geoff Lawson, formerly chief designer at Jaguar, to tell ad people what they are up against in building a global brand:

> There is a Jaguar ethos—values people see as traditional in our cars. You draw a car like this with an eye on the past. You mustn't lose that personality, nor must you let a new car become absorbed within a set of classical lines people have seen before. It's desperately difficult, but it is what we are paid to do.

Importance of Web Advertising, Introduction of New Techniques

Today's ad men and women working with the new digital media find themselves in the position of a carpenter who keeps finding new tools in his toolbox yet is not quite sure how to use them. As the first decade of online advertising comes to a close, the industry's challenge is learning how to make the best use of each technique and devise the best combination of media for each client.

Interactive advertising allows companies to target the people most interested in their brand, based on interests, demographics, behavior, and psychographics, according to the Interactive Advertising's Bureau's (IAB) "Interactive Advertising. At the center of every powerful campaign," an article on the bureau's Web site (http://www.iab.net). The main benefit is that companies can direct ad dollars toward reaching the people most likely to buy their products.

Another advantage that the IAB points out is that interactive media finally allows ad results to measured: "You can accurately and reliably track customer actions and response to your advertising messaging—and then react to customer actions in real-time, something that's not possible with other media. You can track whether an e-mail is opened, whether a video is played, and how long someone interacts with a rich media ad." The bottom line is that the advertiser's return on investment (ROI) can be determined.

Some of the most popular elements of online advertising, according to the IAB, are the following:

Digital video—Allows marketers to combine "the emotional impact of broadcast with the advanced measurement, targeting and accountability of Interactive."

Display—Expandable ads offer additional information to consumers who "mouse over" or click on them, while floating ads attract attention.

E-mail—Best practices in using this tool are "optimizing creative not only for response but also for readability; maintaining a reputation as a responsible and lawful marketer; and managing your programs to make sure your e-mails get delivered."

Online gaming—Advertisers can wrap online games with branding, integrate product placements into the story line, and deliver messages via the "pre-roll" before the game starts.

Lead generation—With interactive media, marketers can collect leads on their Web sites with something as simple as a "Contact Us" form; verify leads using third-party services or on-site software; and follow up with an immediate e-mail recognizing the consumer's interest.

Search—The IAB touts this platform's importance because it allows companies to be listed as part of a consumer's search results and to have the consumer click on the listing and connect directly to the business. Advertisers can bid to show their ads in ranked order when someone searches for a specific word or phrase.

Interactive media can also be used as part of an integrated campaign employing several tools. For instance, suppose an agency had the chance to market a very low-tech product, overalls, an example used by Jack Hitt, a writer for the *New York Times* and the moderator of "Multiscreen Mad Men," a November 23, 2008 panel discussion with three advertising-industry executives. To expand the market for overalls beyond farmers and to "really take the brand into the twenty-first century," Lars Bastholm, creative director at AKQA agency, suggests placing a ShotCode on the front of the garments. Similar to a bar code, a ShotCode can be scanned by cell-phone camera to show the use of a digital display.

"So you'd be wearing a pair of overalls, and you have your own personal ShotCode on the front," Bastholm explains. "The ShotCode might take people online to a new Web site you've selected. Or a picture you took that day or your favorite song. All of a sudden you have a uniquely personalizable pair of overalls that can say something different about you on a daily basis. You'd utilize a whole bunch of screens that we haven't really seen used in clothes before..."

To target the campaign, Benjamin Palmer, CEO of Barbarian Group, suggests ads appealing to the over-40 buyer on social networks like MySpace and a "special edition" just for Facebook users. "They come precoded with your Facebook page embedded at your ShotCode," Palmer explains. "It's self-selecting, actually. The more narrowly you talk to your audience through these new screens, the more people and products will gravitate toward one another."

And that's not all. Robert Rasmussen, executive creative director at the R/GA agency, recommends

> a Web presence built around a utility that engages consumers
> and allows them to take your brand and own it. Maybe you give
> customers the ability to mix and match your overalls with other
> clothes. Maybe you create a widget that lets you drag your overalls
> and drop them onto an existing image. And the program blends the
> overalls with the outfit, so you can say, "Boom, that's how it would
> look if I wore a pair of cord overalls with a blue jean jacket."

Other ideas proposed by the panel include a viral engine that allows customers to drag a photo of a pair of overalls onto a picture of someone in the news; a Web site with a mobile application enabling users to send in a picture of someone and get it back with that person in overalls; and a gallery on this site where visitors can comment and vote on their favorites.

This hypothetical ad campaign underscores the very real trend of focusing on how customers choose to view various media and interact with brands. The very nature of an ad agency is changing, as Bastholm points out: "At my company, we're starting to redefine ourselves from being an ad agency to being an entertainment and technology company." The clients themselves are less enchanted with producing and placing the traditional, expensive 30-second commercial and more interested in the promises of digital media. Bastholm quotes Trevor Edwards, head of Nike's marketing, "'Nike's not in the business of keeping media companies alive, we're in the business of connecting with consumers.'" Rasmussen summarizes the change of mind-set: "Clients are not saying, 'Make us ads' or

'Make us Web sites,' they're saying, 'Create interaction between our brand and our customers.'"

Social Media Marketing: Potential versus Performance

The MySpace and Facebook sites that these ad executives referred to are just two of the many instances of social media, where customers' "conversations" are expected to turn up the volume in coming years. "Now it's about engaging customers in conversation and managing relationships online," according to IPG Emerging Media Labs, as reported by Diane Mermigas in MediaPostNews Marketing Daily (http://www.mediapost.com/publications). Individuals participating in these networks must consider the consequence that "How you represent yourself online determines how friends, employers and the world in general view you." As participants in these networks review products, read blogs, and join online peer communities, attentive companies and marketers can listen to the conversation and learn how to improve service and products. The result, Mermigas writes, is "Social media is becoming the new CRM. The new ROI is Return on Involvement."

Social media also contribute to the "transmission effect," as Mermigas labels the "speed with which conversations and content spread everywhere like rapid fire—beyond the reach of editorial controls, sites or institutions." Armed with such devices as Twitter and instantaneous mobile video on their phones, these savvy networkers challenge brands to stay abreast of "every stage of the conversation" and even be prepared to "manage viral insurrections," according to Mermigas.

In their first ventures into social media, advertisers found that actually selling their wares was much more difficult than conversing about them. In a December 14, 2008 article on the experiences of Procter & Gamble, the world's largest advertiser, with marketing on Facebook, the world's largest social network, Randall Stross, of the *New York Times*, talks to independent experts observing the companies results and concludes, "Members of social networks want to spend time with friends, not brands." Looking into the practice of network members passing along an ad to a friend, Stross cites a 2008 study by IDC, a technology research firm, that found just three percent of Internet users in the United States would be willing to let publishers use their friends for advertising.

Looking specifically at a Procter & Gamble brand page for Tide on Facebook, an 11-month-old campaign where members can post their "favorite places to enjoy stain-making moments," he found just 18 submissions, including two from P&G.

Stross says that advertisers on Facebook have two alternatives: "They can be more intrusive, but the outcome will not be positive. Or they can create genuinely entertaining commercials, but spend ungodly sums to do so."

In the *BusinessWeek* article "Debunking Six Social Media Myths (http://www.businessweek.com), B. L. Ochman provides more reasons why social-networking advertisers shouldn't be too optimistic about their business plans. The myths whose validity he questions are that social-media advertising is cheap, doable by most anyone, likely to "make a big splash in a short time," can be done entirely in-house, will be discovered if it's "great," and cannot be measured.

Though many of the tools used in social media are free, "integrating these tools into a corporate marketing program requires skill, time, and money," Ochman states. Though there may be a few thousand people in digital advertising claiming to be experts, "you'd be hard-pressed to find half a dozen with real track records." Social-media campaigns can garner big results quickly, but usually for companies that already have an established online presence. The "strategy, contacts, tools, and expertise" for pulling off such a campaign is "a combination not generally found in in-house teams, who often reinvent the wheel or use the wrong tools," he writes. "There's no way around having to drive traffic to your social-media site," Ochman insists, preferably though "word of mouse," and you can readily measure your success by blog and other media mentions, real-time blog ad results, click-throughs to the advertiser's Web site, and "very precise statistics" from a number of Web sites.

Though the tools are at hand, Ochman concludes, the experts who know how to use and interpret them are in demand.

Going Mobile

One of the newer media that will be increasingly used in interactive campaigns is mobile devices. In an article on top innovations of 2008 in *AdWeek* (http://www.adweek.com), Mike Shields credits the iPhone with changing the American consumer's mind-set from "'Why would I want to surf the Web on my crappy phone?'

to 'I can do that? I want one now!'" The iPhone's touch screen has been adapted in other new phone models and helps provide advertisers with "a real canvas to play on in the near future, one that goes beyond short-code messages and clunky WAP [wireless application protocol] sites."

These high-tech phones have become a very popular medium for using Twitter, the social-networking and micro-blogging service that enables its users to send and read other users' text-based posts of up to 140 characters in length. Online retailers are using Twitter to alert shoppers to deals, according to the *Wall Street Journal* (http://www.wsj.com), and the sites of companies like The Gap, Target, and Amazon launched wireless-outreach programs in 2008. Kraft's iFood Assistant, an example of a more informational application that helps iPhone users with household chores, offers the kind of "win-win" marketing that brands are seeking in the digital age, according to Emily Bryson York in "Kraft Hits on Killer App for iPhone Marketing," *Advertising Age* (http://www.adage.com). The application offers consumers recipe tips and help creating shopping lists, while providing feedback to Kraft on what they are buying.

With new mobile devices and platforms such as the iPhone and Google Android improving the search and Web experience, "the device consumers search from will start to matter even more than which engine they use," according to David Berkowitz's "Search Trends To Watch In 2009" post of December 23, 2008 on Search Insider blog (http://www.mediapost.com). Marketers can take advantage of this trend by upgrading messaging and landing pages and tailoring their search campaigns to mobile-device features like text messaging, click-to-call, and mobile coupons, Berkowitz suggests.

New Agency Models and Creative Techniques

The proliferation of new media and marketing options has not only led to new strategies among established agencies, but has also given rise to new kinds of agencies.

Founded in 2000 and based in London, Naked Communications eschews the standard creative, planning, and account departments of most ad agencies and instead focuses solely on the "raw ideas" implied in its name, according to Mark Tungate in *Adland*. Naked's founders explain that traditional agencies charge for the execution and "give away" strategy; they, on the other hand, charge clients for

▼

Keeping
in Touch

The Lowdown on LinkedIn

LinkedIn (http://www linkedin.com) can be considered as Facebook for professionals, even though some of them also keep track of Facebook friends on the site that started as the turf of students. LinkedIn doesn't have the same risks of unwanted exposure as Facebook does for some members, but there are some guidelines to follow in building a professional network on the site.

For the article "LinkedIn: Five Dos and Don'ts," posted on The Industry Standard (http://www.thestandard.com), C. G. Lynch invited online identity consultant Kirsten Dixson to act as a high-tech Emily Post outlining LinkedIn etiquette. Some of her key points are:

Profile pictures should be taken by a professional photographer (for about $200 to $250) or, if done at home, shot with a neutral background and very good lighting. Considering how many professional contacts will view the prominent photo, paying a pro seems like a good investment. Dixson cautions against the use of Photoshop to doctor an image, since potential employers who view it should not be surprised when they meet a job candidate.

Like a good headline in a news story or ad, the profile's summary section should be concise and draw people in to read about your accomplishments and expertise. "You want to show who you are, what you do, and why it's unique," Dixson says.

Since your profile is likely to be viewed by associates from the past, it should be completely factual. And because a wide range of people will be seeing it, the profile should include experiences and

creative thinking alone, believing that makes it more valuable. They utilize the mushrooming media channels, selecting "the appropriate channel and the right moment," and ideally allowing the consumer to interact.

Joining Naked Communications in the ideas market are two agencies from two sides of the globe. Anomaly, in New York, generates ideas not only for campaigns but also for products, packaging, and launching, Tungate points out. "It creates intellectual property strengths that will be interesting to "a few different sectors of your industry," Dixson suggested. Including words that people are likely to use for Google searches increases the chances of being seen on LinkedIn; yet they can only view a profile if the account is set to "public."

In her blog post "LinkedIn Etiquette," Penelope Trunk (http://www.blog.penelopetrunk.com) says that a profile should be more "chatty" than a resume. "More cocktail party than job interview," she wrote.

There are two schools of thought on how to choose connections on LinkedIn, according to Lynch. LinkedIn officially states that only known contacts should be added as connections, since they reflect on you professionally. Others consider themselves LinkedIn Open Networkers (LIONS), who add people as connections whether they know them or not so they can build their networks. Dixson recommends setting guidelines in between these two extremes; for instance, always giving a reason for a declining a connection. Instead of the canned invitation of "I'd like to add you as a connection," a note of introduction could prompt the invitee to remember the sender. But Trunk says that it's fine to send the site's standard invitation to people you know, because it's understood that everyone is busy.

For the recommendations section of the site, Dixson suggests a "360" approach that includes input from people who worked with the profiler in several capacities. And on LinkedIn as in all social networking, she points out, "...what goes around comes around. If you go and write a good recommendation for a colleague, odds are someone will do the same for you in the future."

that it then licenses to clients in return for a share of revenue." Australian creative director Dave Droga has an even more expansive of view of idea generating.

His agency, Droga5, offers clients "creative communications" that can involve "entertainment, architecture, community and online," as he told *Campaign* in an interview quoted by Tungate. For example, his viral Internet campaign for Marc Ecko's clothing showed grainy footage of a graffiti writing "Still free" on what appeared to be Air Force One.

Some other agencies in the United States have come up with innovative ideas to boost their own business. They are applying their hard-earned expertise in marketing clients' products to promoting products of their own.

The ad agency Brooklyn Brothers makes Fat Pig chocolate, and the British agency Bartle Bogle Hagerty has launched a division called Zag dedicated to creating new brands, like a personal security device and a line of vegetarian meals, according to the *New York Times* article, "Ad Agencies Fashion Their Own Horn, And Toot It," published December 30, 2008. But perhaps their most popular venture in the U. S. has been the blog Mrs. O (http://mrs-o.org), which tracks the outfits worn by Michelle Obama and highlights the designers and retailers where the first lady obtained them.

Reversing the usual ad-agency practice on Mrs. O, Zag sells ad space instead of buying it, the *New York Times* reports. George Parker, an ad agency consultant and writer of the blog AdScam, told the *New York Times* that Zag's business model has important implications for advertising's future, predicting that "the creation of intellectual property and new products is something you're going to see a lot more of." Besides being a source of revenue for agencies, Parker added, ventures like Mrs. O allow them to show clients that they have an expertise beyond agencies' traditional services.

Offline Innovations: Alternative Advertising

All the parking spaces in front of the Town Hall in Madrid, Spain, are taken, several of them by cars that are "parked" vertically, their trunks high in the air. "Wouldn't it have been better if you'd left the car at home?" says a sign near them.

A smoker in one of Singapore's public spots reaches to flick her ashes in an ashtray, and then is taken aback by seeing it looks like unhealthy human lungs.

Walking down a street in Belgium, pedestrians hear screams coming from one of the grates. When they get up close to the grate and look down, they read a sign saying, "Today 133 journalists are imprisoned and tortured all over the world."

These are examples of alternative advertisements for, respectively, a Day Without Cars, the Singapore Cancer Society, and Reporters Without Borders. They all appear in the book *Advertising Is Dead, Long Live Advertising!* by Tom Himpe. The "dead" in Himpe's title refers to his premise that there are "too many advertisers using the same channels to reach the same people at the same time." So he documents the new types of ads that have appeared around the world during the last decade.

Grouped in categories like "Infiltration," "Installation," and "Transformation," the techniques sometimes sound more relevant to warfare than to advertising. In fact, Himpe discusses the practice of "guerilla advertising." Yet if overused conventional advertising doesn't work, how effective are these alternatives? Himpe suggests evaluating them by the criteria of "proximity, exclusivity, invisibility and unpredictability" and trusting that "a gut feeling and some basic consumer research can shed light on which ideas of channels are winners and which are not."

That assessment of alternative advertising might not sit too well with corporate marketers who will always have to watch the bottom line.

Key Industry Events

ADDY Awards   Billed as the world's largest advertising competition with over 60,000 entries in 2009, ADDYs are administered by the American Advertising Federation.   (http://www.aaf.org/default.asp?id=27)

Advertising Research Foundation Convention & Expo   A key forum for keeping up with the latest research in advertising and marketing.   (http://www.thearf.org)

American Association of Advertising Agencies' Annual Media Conference & Trade Show   The main event of this premier advertising trade association is organized around a popular theme, such as "Digital Changes Everything" in 2008.   (http://www.aaaa.org—see Events)

The Cannes Lions International Advertising Festival   Organized around the presentation of the prestigious Cannes Lion awards for creative work, the festival is attended by thousands of industry insiders from nearly 100 countries.   (http://www.canneslions.com)

Direct Marketing Association National Convention   Offers over 100 educational sessions and discussions plus the world's largest exhibition for direct and interactive marketers.   (http://www.the-dma.org—see Upcoming Events & Seminars)

Effies Awards   Focused on "Ideas That Work," Effies recognize a broad range of advertising, including print, TV, packaging design, guerrilla marketing, events, and digital.   (http://www.effie.org)

National Retail Federation Convention & Expo   Is known as "Retail's BIG Show," this event attracts top retailers from all over the world.   (http://www.nrf.org—see Events & Conferences)

New York Advertising Week   A combination of the latest industry ideas and special-event programming that brings together clients, creatives, media professionals, and entertainers.   (http://www.advertisingweek.com)

OBIE Awards   OBIEs recognize excellence in outdoor advertising. (http://www.aef.com/exhibits/awards/obie_awards)

Major Industry Associations

The Advertising Council (also Ad Council)   Since its founding in 1942 the Ad Council has created a wide array of public service advertising.   (http://www.adcouncil.org)

Advertising Research Foundation   An open forum for the exchange of ideas and research strategies, the ARF offers access to extensive online resources and personal assistance.   (http://www.thearf.org)

American Advertising Federation   Billing itself as the "Unifying Voice for Advertising," the AAF is a national advertising trade association representing 40,000 professionals in the industry. (http://www.aaf.org)

American Association of Advertising Agencies   Founded in 1917, the AAAA is a national trade association representing the advertising industry. Its membership produces approximately 80 percent of the total advertising volume placed by agencies nationwide.   (http://www.aaaa.org)

American Marketing Association   The largest marketing association in North America, the AMA has nearly 40,000 members including academics, researchers, and practitioners.   (http://www.marketingpower.com)

Interactive Advertising Bureau   Comprised of nearly 400 media and technology companies responsible for selling almost 90% of online advertising in the United States, the IAB focuses on the growth of the interactive advertising marketplace.   (http://www.iab.net)

Major Players

Lee Clow, TBWA/Chiat/Day *Advertising Age* has called Clow "advertising's art director guru." (http://www.tbwachiat.com)

Nina DiSesa, Chairman, McCann Erickson New York DiSesa was the first woman and the first creative director to be made chairman in the McCann global network. She is also the author of *Seducing the Boys Club: Uncensored Tactics from a Woman at the Top.* (http://www.mccan.com)

David Droga, Founder, droga5 After becoming the first worldwide creative director for Publicis Worldwide in 2003, Droga went on to lead a joint venture with the Publicis Group called droga5, a brand ideas and entertainment laboratory. (http://www.droga5.com)

Jean-Marie Dru, Chairman, TBWAWorldwide Former CEO of Young & Rubicam in Paris, Dru was appointed president and CEO worldwide of TBWAWorldwide in 2001. In 2008 he became chairman. (http://www.tbwa.com)

Sir John Hegarty, Chairman & Worldwide Creative Director, BartleBogleHegarty World-renowned creator of famous ad campaigns for Levi's, Lego, and Audi, Hegarty heads one the most acclaimed agencies. (http://www.bbh.co.uk)

David Kennedy, Co-Founder, Wieden + Kennedy The highly successful agency's co-founding partner. (http://www.wk.com)

Washington Olivetto, Chairman, W/Brasil A creative director with a pop-star status in Brazilian media, Olivetto created the famous campaign for BomBril that is included in the Guiness Book of Records as the campaign longest on the air with the same lead character (more than 160 commercials over the last sixteen years). (http://www.wbrasil.com.br)

Marcello Serpa, Co-CEO & Creative Director, Almap/BBDO, Brazil Throughout his career, Serpa has been known as Brazil's most honored art director, having won top prizes in the principal Brazilian and international advertising festivals. (http://www.almapbbdo.com.br)

Martin Sorrell, WPP Group Joined the large British advertising conglomerate WPP in 1986 as a director, becoming the Group's chief executive in the same year. (http://www.wpp.com)

Dan Wieden, Co-Founder, Wieden + Kennedy Co-founded one of the first major agencies in the Northwest, which became known for breakthrough creative work. (http://www.wk.com)

Top U.S. Ad Agencies

BBDO   Part of the OmniCom Group, BBDO's clients have included Pepsi, Best Buy, and Chrysler.   (http://www.bbdo.com)

Campbell-Ewald   Touting its Detroit roots, the agency has worked for such major brands as General Motors, Carrier , and the United States Postal Service.   (http://www.campbell-ewald.com)

DDB   The clients of DDB (Dane, Doyle, Bernbach) have included Volkswagen, Fox, McDonald's, and Hasbro Monopoly.   (http://www.ddb.com)

Grey   Grey Group's clients have included Sara Lee, Kraft, and Toshiba.   (http://www.grey.com)

JWT   Founded as the J. Walter Thompson agency, JWT has provided advertising for Jetblue, Ford, Nestle, and many other companies.   (http://www.jwt.com)

McCann Erickson   One of seven marketing communications companies in McCann Worldgroup, McCann Erickson's clients have included Coca-Cola, the U.S. Army, and Mastercard.   (http://www.mccann.com)

Ogilvy & Mather   Founded by the legendary adman David Ogilvy, the agency's clients have included Adidas, IBM, and Greenpeace.   (http://www.ogilvy.com)

Y&R Advertising   Originally Young & Rubicam, Y&R has worked for such major brands as Land Rover, Virgin Atlantic, and Converse.   (http://www.yr.com)

Current Trends in Public Relations

Inbound Marketing

The Internet is changing the public relations industry, too. The first "Inbound Marketing Summit" held in Boston, in 2008, alerted pubic-relations professionals to the importance of this new Web-based marketing in their industry. While traditional or outbound marketing focuses on finding customers, according to Rick Burnes, writing on Hubspot's Inbound Internet Marketing Blog (http://www.blog.hubspot.com), inbound marketing helps companies get found by customers.

Burns cites three components of successful inbound marketing: Web content that is interesting enough to attract potential customers to a Web site; effective search engine optimization (SEO), or building a Web site and the inbound links to it to maximize ranking in search engines, where most customers find sites; and targeting social media, where marketing "becomes more authentic and nuanced, and is more likely to draw qualified customers to your site."

Writing on his Web site's blog, Paul Roetzer, founder and president of PR 20/20 (http://www.pr2020.com/blog), says the types of content for inbound marketing include "blogs, podcasts, videos, optimized press releases, case studies, white papers, e-books, and by-lined articles." An update of an essential PR tool, optimized press releases are keyword-rich, electronic documents designed to generate inbound links to a Web site, while reaching targeted audiences.

Social Media Fosters New Relations with the Public

As in advertising, burgeoning social media are transforming public relations, too.

Some of the new media's influence was addressed on the "Inside the Entrepreneurial Mind" series on Openforum.com, hosted by Seth Godin. "The traditional wisdom was that biz should direct the relationship, through a PR person," says Sean Parker, founder of Facebook. "But now, the person in the company whom the blogger wrote about should respond directly to the blogger. Bloggers are influential now as they are read by the traditional media. Also, Facebook members' comments are often picked up by the blogosphere."

"Facebook hosts micro-communities," Godin adds. "Company news doesn't have to be read by everybody; it can be focused on a subgroup, like those who want catgut strings used for tennis rackets."

The third panel member, Jimmy Wales, founder of Wikipedia, says, "Hosting a conversation builds brand loyalty, plus you find out a whole lot about your customers from the conversation. Sometimes you get criticisms that are hard to hear. But people are going to talk about your brand anyway, so you might as well know what they're saying and respond."

In a 2008 speech posted on the Institute for Public Relations Web site (http://www.insittuteforpr.com), Sir Martin Sorrell, group chief executive, WPP, defines PR's role in the era when everyone can speak out on the Web: "In all this clutter and fragmentation, it falls to Public Relations professionals to lead companies into this conversation between mainstream media, employees, analysts, investors, bloggers, and competitors around brands." But Sir Sorrell cautions that you can't "spin your way into a blogger's heart." Instead, he cites the

INTERVIEW

Gaining Insight into Customers

Jon Steel

Author, *Truth, Lies & Advertising: The Art of Account Planning*;
Perfect Pitch: The Art of Selling Ideas and Winning New Business;
and new business training consultant at WPP

In *Perfect Pitch* you talk about "the art of influencing people by storytelling," particularly in presentations. Is storytelling becoming a trend in advertising? What are some of its current applications?

Brand building has always been about storytelling. The world's greatest and most enduring brands are in that position because they told good stories from the start, and have succeeded in keeping them interesting. Of course a lot of other stuff is necessary to sustain a brand's health, but without a compelling story, well told, there is little chance of sustained success.

Account planning has been part of the industry for 40 years now. How has the practice developed over the years and what are some the "best practices" in planning that you would point out today?

The best practices in planning today are the best practices of 40 years ago. Great planners ask the questions about consumers' attitudes toward products that others fail to ask; they are good listeners; they are not afraid of saying "no" when work is not good enough, and they are tireless in their support when naysayers threaten the life of a potentially great idea.

You wrote *Truth, Lies & Advertising* before the Internet came to the fore in advertising. Has that medium significantly changed the way agencies do planning? For instance, do they read consumers' blog comments as a way of listening to them.

The Internet has changed many things, but it should not change the way that agencies do planning. At its core, planning is about understanding and influencing the relationships between people and brands, and as the Internet has changed those relationships, so too should planning adapt. It should not, however, be an excuse for planners to neglect their research responsibilities, to stop meeting members of their target audience face-to-face, to pass off sloppy, unedited streams-of-consciousness opinions as "Big Thinking." Too many planners are spending too much time blogging and relying on others' blogs for their information. If they were working in my department I would fire them.

Are there still good opportunities in planning for people entering the business? Any suggestions for how to get a first job in planning and then advancing one's career in this role?
There are still many good opportunities, but not enough agencies are hiring smart graduates and training them as planners. My advice to any aspiring young planner is to choose a mentor rather than an agency, because most great planners were helped early in their career by someone older and wiser.

At the 2007 Verge London conference on "Listening," you mentioned the importance of new ways of listening to consumers, and new ways of responding to what agencies hear. Would you expand on these new approaches?
I was simply referring to our ability to engage with people in ways that would have seemed in the realms of science fiction when I was a young planner. However, being able to listen to people in new ways doesn't mean that we should. Agencies love being the first to develop a campaign using some new technology, but in my opinion there's still no substitute for talking to people the old-fashioned way.

At this same conference you mentioned "leading without seeming to" and "influencing from within, not from without." Please explain those strategies and give some examples.
Both advertising and planning generally work best when people don't notice that they are being influenced. I could cite dozens of examples, but in the end it's a question of human nature. We do things more willingly when we believe we are doing so of our own volition, and not because we are being coerced. Anyone who doesn't understand this will never make a good planner.

Perfect Pitch **offers good advice for improving the way presentations are made in the business. How can recent graduates, trained in relying on PowerPoint and other technology, gain the confidence to start making human connections and adding a personal element to their presentations?**
Recent graduates probably have lots of experience making connections and influencing people, even though this experience may not

(continues on next page)

INTERVIEW

Gaining Insight into Customers (continued)

come from the world of business. I assume they will have previously conducted successful financial communications with their parents, and most will have used their understanding of the human psyche to attract partners. They simply need to bring these instincts to business. If they are forced to use PowerPoint, there's no law that says they have to use it as badly as 99 percent of other business people. With a little imagination, even a PowerPoint presentation can be memorable and effective.

In his book *Advertising Is Dead, Long Live Advertising*, **Tom Himpe writes: "Old methods don't work because conventional channels are blocked because so many advertisers are using them to reach the same people at the same time." So he recommends "experiential marketing" like staged events, installations, and intrusion (for instance,** *The Economist* **placing ads right on gym equipment in Singapore: "Raise the bar," "Get off the treadmill"). What do you think of these new ways of involving consumers?**

example of Dell Computer, whose executives invited customers to post their comments online, creating "a real-time focus group—free of charge." Dell did not censor negative comments but reorganized their customer service to respond to them. The result? "Within two years," Sir Sorrell says, "Dell had halved negative online chatter about its products."

Another sign that social networking is taking hold in public relations is that the industry's media are discussing "best practices" in the new area, as Roxanna Guilford-Blake did in "Six Essential Steps of Building a Digital Brand," published on The Firm Voice (http://firmvoice.com). One useful practice is Coyne PR's "45-1 rule," which requires that staff spend at least 45 minutes becoming familiar with a blogger before starting a conversation with him or her, Guilford-Blake suggests. Staff should also be active participants in social media, as they are at Coyne, where everyone has a blog or contributes to one

The Economist example you cite is very similar to much of the work GS&P did for the "got milk?" campaign in California, putting "got milk?" on checkout dividers, on grocery carts, and even on bananas. But that stuff worked because it was part of a bigger campaign, which included the "old methods" like TV, print, and outdoor that Tom Himpe rejects. I have heard people say that Nike demonstrates the superiority of new media over old, with its design-your-own shoe site. Yes, it's a good site, but would it work without the 30 years of fantastic "old" advertising that Nike has done and continues to do? The question for traditional media isn't whether it works or not, but how can it work better in conjunction with some of the new media now at our disposal? And I think you'll find that the smartest marketers, including Nike, have been taking this approach for at least the last 25 years.

People starting out in advertising usually have to "pay their dues" by working long hours and always being connected to the office. Yet in *Perfect Pitch* you make a strong case for "creating room for thought." How would you advise ambitious, hardworking people in entry-level jobs to strike that balance between work and personal time?
By learning the importance of the word "no." And by producing the kind of top-quality work that makes others question their own working practices.

and "90 percent are involved in social networks, 78 percent are on Facebook, 93 percent are on LinkedIn, and 64 percent tweet on Twitter." Guilford-Blake points to Coyne staffers who work with bloggers writing on specific topics, like "mom bloggers" and automotive bloggers. "They've cultivated relationships in those sectors," she writes. "They read the blogs. They know the people writing them. And they listen, to discover what the bloggers think, do and want, allowing them to customize content—and avoid embarrassing missteps."

Changing Relationship Between PR and the Media

As the Internet becomes increasingly prominent and print journalism declines, it stands to reason that public relations' interactions with the media are changing. In a November 20, 2008 post on his blog The Tweney Review (http://dylan.tweney.com), "Journalism and PR in the New Media Age," Dylan F. Tweney analyzes these changes and tries to clarify the roles of these two industries:

> The traditional relationship between journalists and PR people is in flux because PR people are no longer as dependent upon journalists as they used to be. When a company can deliver its press release directly to the public via PR Newswire and a wide network of bloggers, the press no longer have exclusive control over the channels of public communication. When reporters at traditional media outlets compete with hundreds of bloggers for PR people's attention, the press can't count on getting the time and attention they used to get....

Among the suggestions he gives for the establishment of new relations between PR and the press is that "PR people are potential allies in the search for news. They are also adversaries in that they have their client's agenda in mind, and will want the story told (or not told) in a certain way. But they can be useful sources of information, and in some areas, such as new product announcements, they are indispensable." The old "gentleman's agreement" on embargoes for new product launches has gone the way of the typewriter, Tweney says, as bloggers were never partner to them and have no incentive to start the practice now.

Tweney also gives PR practitioners a word to the wise on the best way to get information to journalists, "who are under massive time pressure because of the quantity of information we need to digest and the quantity of stories we are expected to produce. As a result, most of us do not welcome phone calls of any kind—especially the 'did you get the e-mail I just sent?' variety. Phone calls interrupt our workflow and are more time-consuming to deal with than e-mails; plus they don't allow the PR person to convey as much information as an e-mail message."

High-Tech Press Release

If Edward Bernays could see how much the traditional press release has changed in recent years, it could make the Father of Spin's head spin. Formerly a paper document, the traditional PR tool has now become a video news release (VNR) that can be distributed to journalists via satellite or other broadband technologies, according to John Pavlik in "Mapping the Consequences of Technology on Public

Relations," published on the Institute for Public Relations Web site (http://www.instituteforpr.org). VNRs can be tracked by electronic systems like SIGMA from Nielsen Media Research, which reports that the system can record each airing across the country with over 95 percent accuracy, Pavlik writes.

In the foreseeable future, VNRs are expected to be viewable on portable devices such as mobile phones, and will reach their audiences without being sent to news channels, according to Pavlik. The videos are already available on sites like YouTube and can be easily found through search engines like Google. PR practitioners can also better determine the extent of their VNRs' use through new research technology like TeleTrax.

In addition to helping PR agencies get their own messages seen and heard, new digital technology is also making it possible to monitor the reporting of dozens of online news sources. Pavlik cites Columbia Newsblaster as an effective system for tracking and synthesizing news coverage of topics, organizations, and people. For a broader perspective, Google Trends tracks search queries both nationally and worldwide, providing the search volume of specific terms with data sorted by cities, regions, and languages. And as an example of the fast digital pace that PR practitioners must keep up with, the technology article includes an example of one technical advance giving rise to another: Google Alerts can be used to monitor the traffic on blogs.

Key Industry Events

Arthur W. Page Society Annual Conference The main event of this society specifically for senior PR practitioners and corporate communication executives.   (http://www.awpagesociety.com)

Association for Education in Journalism & Mass Communication (AEJMC) Convention Brings together faculty, administrators, students, and media professionals from journalism and mass communication.   (http://www.aejmc.org/_events/convention)

International Association of Business Communicators World Conference Drawing from over 80 countries, this conference is for all professions that represent companies with the media. (http://www.iabc.com)

International Public Relations Research Conference Presented in conjunction with the University of Miami and other sponsors, it is billed as the only conference devoted entirely to research in public relations.   (http://www.instituteforpr.org/bss_info/iprrc_main)

Public Relations Executive Forum Limited to 35 registrants, the forum is intended to develop the future leaders in PR and corporate communications. (http://www.instituteforpr.org/education/executive_forum)

Public Relations Society of America's International Conference—The four-day conference has offered over 80 professional development sessions on industry trends. (http://www.prsa.com/conferences)

Major Associations

Arthur W. Page Society Founded especially for senior PR practitioners and corporate communication executives. (http://www.awpagesociety.com)

Boston College Center for Corporate Citizenship A resource for professionals to learn about PR's role in improving the social, environmental, and economic well-being of companies and society. (http://www.bcccc.net)

Center for Media and Democracy Promotes transparency and an informed debate by, according to the group's Web site, "exposing corporate spin and government propaganda" and by engaging the public in accurate reporting. (http://www.prwatch.org)

Council of Communication Management For senior communications practitioners committed to helping each other and their organizations succeed. (http://www.ccmconnection.com)

Council of Public Relations Firms Founded in 1998 as the first national association representing the interests of public relations firms. (http://www.prfirms.org)

Institute for Public Relations Focused on research-based knowledge in public relations and making this knowledge available to practitioners, educators, researchers, and their clients. (http://www.instituteforpr.org)

National Investor Relations Institute Association of corporate officers and investor relations consultants who communicate among corporate management, shareholders, securities analysts, and others in the financial community. (http://www.niri.org)

Public Affairs Council Launched in 1954 at the urging of President Dwight D. Eisenhower, the council provides information, training, and other resources to support effective participation in government, community. and public relations. (http://www.pac.org)

Public Relations Society of America Chartered in 1947, PRSA endeavors to advance the standards of the public-relations profession and to provide continuing education programs, informational forums, and research projects. (http://www.prsa.org)

Major Players

Harold Burson, Chairman, Burson-Marstellar With more than 50 years in the business, Burson was described as "the century's most influential PR figure" in a survey conducted by *PRWeek*. (http://www.burson-marsteller.com)

Keith Burton, President, Insidedge Formerly chief client officer and regional managing director at Golin/Harris, Burton is president of Insidedge, specializing in employee trust and corporate structure. (http://www.insidedge.net)

Ofield Dukes, President, Ofield Dukes & Assoc. A communications consultant for every Democratic presidential campaign since 1972, Dukes is also the founder of the Black Public Relations Society of Washington. (http://www.ofield.com)

Jack Felton, CEO Emeritus, Institute for Public Relations Formerly vice president for corporate communications at McCormick Co. Inc., Felton teaches in the University of Florida's School of Journalism and Communications. (http://www.instituteforpr.org)

Marilyn Laurie, President, Laurie Consulting Formerly executive vice president of public relations at AT&T, Laurie is a recipient of *Inside PR*'s Lifetime Achievement award.

Betsy Plank, Principal, Betsy Plank Public Relations Plank is often referred to as the "first lady" of public relations. The University of Alabama's Plank Center for Leadership in Public Relations is named for her. (http://www.plankcenter.ua.edu/betsy.html)

Top U.S. Public Relations Agencies

Burson-Marsteller Part of Young & Rubicam Brands, the agency's clients have included IKEA, Hormel Foods, and Century 21. (http://www.burson-marstellar.com)

Edelman Public Relations Worldwide *PR Week's* 2009 Large Agency of the Year, Edelman has provided counsel for Quaker Oats, Brita, and Roche. (http://www.edelman.com)

Fleishman-Hillard A global communications network headquartered in St. Louis, the agency has worked with the American

Veterinary Medical Association, Pulte Homes, and the Library of Congress.   (http://www.fleishman.com)

Hill & Knowlton Part of communications giant WWP and with offices in over 40 countries, Hill & Knowlton's clients have included Smithsonian National Museum, Procter & Gamble, and Labatt Breweries.   (http://www.hillandknowlton.com)

Ketchum Communications Merging with the German PR leader Pleon in 2009, Ketchum's clients have included Kodak, FedEx, and Roche.   (http://www.ketchum.com)

Publicis Consultants-PR The agency's clients have included ZOLL Medical Corporation, Sodastream, and Subway.   (www.publicisconsultants-pr.com)

Weber Shandwick The agency's clients have included General Motors, Microsoft, and Electrolux.   (http://www.webershandwick.com)

Chapter 3

On the Job

There are many roles to fill within the world of advertising and public relations. Whether you have a gift for design, a facility with language, or an ability to work with numbers and financial data, there is a place for you. What follows is a thorough listing of the various careers available in the industry today, complete with job descriptions, educational and professional prerequisites, and examples of day-to-day responsibilities. Let this information help gauge your most effective points of entry into the field of advertising.

Advertising

Account Management Department

Account Executive
As the go-between for the agency and the client, the account executive (or AE) probably has the most multifaceted job in advertising. To perform it well, she must lead like a quarterback, negotiate like a diplomat, and keep her eye on the big picture like the executive she is. Oh, yes: and do it all on budget.

The account executive works with colleagues from all the other areas of the agency: creative, media, research, production, and sometimes public relations. The goal is to motivate all these team members to "give the client their best effort without spending more time than the income from the client's business justifies," according to the Advertising Educational Foundation Web site (http://www.aef.com). Just as important, the account executive must have a broad-based knowledge of the client's business, the consumer, and the competition.

This go-between obtains a good understanding of the client's objectives, communicates them to the creative and media staffs, and presents recommendations for the campaign to the client. Accomplishing all of this means that the account executive's day is varied, stimulating, often hectic, and sometimes downright stressful.

In the course of a typical day an account executive might talk to a client's staff about a campaign that is currently running, an approval for a proposed ad, and selecting a producer for an upcoming commercial. Then he might meet with his agency's creative staff about a brief for an upcoming campaign, question an over-budget expense, and let them know about his attempts to get a client approval that they need. Later in the day the AE might field a question from a media-planning colleague about the client's desire to run an ad during expensive commercial time, and then call the client to talk diplomatically about spending less on running the ad.

Learning the ropes in the accounts department and working to be promoted to a full-fledged AE are junior account executives. Account executives can work their way up to be senior account executives.

Management titles in this department are: account director (or director of client services), who runs the department and is responsible for profit and loss and strategic leadership; group account director, who manages one large account or several smaller ones; management supervisor, who is responsible for the overall service and profitability of an account and represents the agency's senior management on a daily basis with the client; and account supervisor, who provides strategic recommendations and manages all agency resources to satisfy the client.

Account Planning Department

Account Planner

While account management is dedicated to serving the client, account planning is focused on understanding the customer. Of course the two areas are closely related in their common goal: planning's insights into customers' desires and behavior help produce more effective ads that yield greater sales, which will surely please the client.

To put it simply, planners try to "get inside customers' heads" to find out what "turns them on." But the discipline is much more complicated and subtle than that. Planners do such extensive field-work among consumers that they are sometimes called cognitive anthropologists, or "cogs." Besides conducting interviews and focus groups, planners go right to consumers' homes and the places they shop to observe "how they use and perceive specific products and services," according to the now defunct Your Big Ideas Web site of the American Association of Advertising Agencies (formerly at http://www.yourbigideas.org).

They also combine this qualitative information with quantitative research, such as a product's sales history, competitors' sales, brand awareness, and consumer demographics. Planners must be skilled at synthesizing the results of all their varied research in a way that is clear to the creative team, who must "execute" based on the findings. But advertising experts agree that the key, underlying characteristic of a good account planner is a strong curiosity about human nature and motivation. Those eternal variables keep their jobs interesting.

In addition to account planner, the most popular title in this department, the American Association of Advertising Agencies Web site (http://www.aaaa.org) describes other planning jobs, including: planning director, the "conscience" of the client's brand and leader of its strategy; associate director account planning, the manager of the planning supervisors, who in turn coaches the planners; and assistant account planners, who do drafting, prep work, and other duties under the guidance of planners.

Double Teaming Accounts

From the time when account planning was imported from England in the early 1980s, there has been some confusion over how it differs from more traditional account management. Bruce Kelley, vice-chairman of the Martin Agency, clarifies the roles of these key advertising positions in two columns posted on the Memos to Account Management section of http://www.aef.org.

Initially most planners in U.S. agencies were former researchers who changed their title, making planning very quantitative, Kelley writes. Eventually planning came into its own with the role of developing creative strategy and understanding the client's brand and its importance. Then as clients realized the value of their brands, the planner became more important to them and to the agency.

The rise of planners "had the de facto effect of diminishing the role of the account manager," according to Kelley. Yet he proposes

Problem
Solving

"The End of the Plain Plane"

Some ad campaigns have such a big impact that they not only boost a company's business, but also transform a whole industry's products and marketing. In 1966, Jack Tinker & Partners' campaign for Braniff Airlines made that kind of splash.

As recounted in her book *A Big Life (In Advertising)*, Tinker partner Mary Wells Lawrence was challenged by the new head of Braniff to come up with a "very big idea" that would fill the seats of the then little known airline's fleet. So Lawrence and her partners visited airports around the country to assess the state of the industry. A vivacious woman with theatrical flair, Lawrence found utilitarian metallic planes, nondescript terminals, and "stewardesses" in nurse-like uniforms.

"This was the sixties, mind you, when color was a hot marketing tool," she writes. She saw Braniff as a blank canvas in need of a zesty palette, and enlisted the design help of Emilio Pucci, known for making flashy women's clothes, and Alexander Girard, designer of the New York restaurant Fonda del Sol, a "high-octane color montage of Mexican and modern."

Together they hit on the idea of introducing colored planes—blue, green, yellow, even a "shimmering turquoise." They spread paper cut-out fleets of all one color on their agency floor and looked them over for a few days. But it wasn't until the Tinker team mixed all seven colors in one fleet of planes that the idea really came to

that account management has now evolved into a new type of job, one much bigger than just supervising the making of ads: becoming "an expert on the client's business."

The benefits of this expertise, according to Kelley, are that it can provide the rationale for why a client should buy great creative work, create client confidence in the agency and therefore strengthen their relationship, give account managers the insight to develop additional client services and thus generate incremental revenue for the agency, and help secure the account by making the account manager an invaluable member of the client's team.

life. The designers also made over the terminals, the check-in area, and stewardess's uniforms to look equally exciting. Pucci, under the impression that all Braniff flights went to areas with warmer weather, suggested the stewardesses remove their sleek uniforms piece by piece in an ad called "The Air Strip."

Braniff knew that Lawrence and company had delivered the requested "big idea" at a debut press conference on an airport run-way, where seven colorful planes flew low over the heads of cheering members of the press from around the world.

"The advertising has to live up to the planes," Lawrence then told Tinker copywriter Charlie Moss and art director Phil Parker. But Moss was so impressed with the airline's glamorous transforma-tion that he got writer's block trying to equal it, and Parker took to drinking martinis at lunch. Then one day Lawrence walked into the unproductive team's office and spotted a layout in their wastebasket.

"Phil had drawn a big orange plane across two pages. On one of the wings he had put the entire Braniff crew in their Pucci uniforms, Alexander Girard's multicolored seats and a 10-piece Mexican band. Charlie had written the headline: 'The end of the plain plane. We don't get you there any faster. It just seems that way.'"

Not only did the campaign put an end to the "plain plane" and change airline advertising and design for good, but also, as Lawrence recalls, "In less than a year we received more publicity in newspapers and magazines than we paid for advertising in over 10 years."

How can account managers learn more about a client's business? Kelley makes several suggestions:

- Periodically take a tour of the client's factory or plant.
- Read all client-related trends, reports, and periodicals.
- Delve into all client research, even if it's not about advertising or the consumer.
- Know how the client goes to market with its product or service.
- Ask to attend some of the client's staff meetings.
- Meet and get to know people in the client organization

beyond the advertising and marketing departments.
- Attend the client's industry trade shows and conventions.
- If the client has a retail store, spend time working in it.
- Ask the client for other ways to increase knowledge of the business.

Creative Department

Many departments in an agency collaborate on ad campaigns. But for the general public, the work produced by copywriters and art directors is what defines advertising: the ads in print and on radio, television, the Internet, and billboards. Even in the business, account managers, planners, and media staff will usually admit that the greatest market plan will fail without the right "creative"—an industry term that can mean the ads themselves in various stages of development, the department where the ads are produced, and the staff members in that department. Of course this work has to satisfy the client, which is why creative always presents several ideas from which the client chooses.

Because their work is highly visible and eligible to be honored by one of the many awards in advertising, it may seem like creatives have the glory jobs in the field. But it is not all fun and prizes, as this quote originally published on the Web site Yourbigideas.org suggests: "...creatives need more than just creativity—they also need patience, resourcefulness and strong communication skills." Many copywriters and art directors would think that statement should win an award for understatement.

The key jobs in creative are as follows:

Art Director

Art directors develop design concepts and review material that is to appear in periodicals, newspapers, and other printed or digital media. They decide how best to present information visually, so that it is eye-catching, appealing, and organized, according to the U. S. Bureau of Labor Statistics' *Occupational Outlook Handbook*. They begin with a layout or broad-stroke sketch of the ad, traditionally on paper but now more often on a computer. For television commercials, instead of a layout they create storyboards, a series of sketches showing what images will be included in the ad, complemented with copy.

Everyone
Knows

The Creative Brief

A team of an art director and a copywriter depend on a creative brief to get their creative wheels spinning. As discussed in the Account Planning section, the creative brief spells out the guidelines for meeting the client's expectations of the ad or of an entire campaign—a series of related ads often run in a number of different media. In *Truth, Lies & Advertising,* Jon Steel writes that the task of a creative briefing, the meeting or meetings that produce the brief or document, is "to inform the creative team, and most important, to inspire them. To reduce all the information that has been gathered from the client, from consumer research, and perhaps many other sources besides, funnel it down to a single, potent idea, and from that idea to create a sense of possibilities, of great advertising just waiting to happen."

Since art directors and copywriters work so closely together, they often get to know each other's jobs very well. Sometimes their partner's work seems so interesting that copywriters want to become art directors, and vice versa. In their book *Pick Me: Breaking Into Advertising and Staying There,* Nancy Vonk and Janet Keslin, co-chief creative directors at Ogilvy & Mather, Toronto, address questions about creative roles. The questions are taken from their column, Ask Jancy, on http://www.ihaveanidea.org, a Web site devoted to the creative side of advertising. An art director with five years' experience and an interest in copywriting asks them if she will have to leave her agency to pursue her career switch. "Jancy," Keslin's and Vonk's combined pen name replies, "Many art directors have made this switch," and suggest first getting an honest opinion on writing skills from other creatives and, if the results are positive, to talk with the agency's creative director about the goal. "A smart CD will see what she can do" for a valued employee, they say, adding that "writer-writer and art director-art director teams are not unheard of, at least for a limited period of time."

Even when looking for a first job, Jancy replies to another question, it's possible to market oneself as an art director and/or copywriter. "Most likely you'll find your heart is in one place or the other and commit to excelling in that discipline," they add.

Art directors decide which photographs or artwork to use and oversee the design, layout, and production of material to be published. They may manage other staff members engaged in artwork, design, and layout.

The "director" part of the job entails selecting and coordinating the best talent to produce the ad, including graphic artists, illustrators, photographers, television producers and crews, and Web designers. Directing also comes into play in photo studios and "on location," the site chosen as the background that will showcase a product effectively. Some art directors develop a signature style of ads that makes them in demand—and sometimes copied.

Art directors may start out at a junior level and progress to a senior role, and often aspire to become a creative director.

Copywriter

Complementing the work of the art director, copywriters supply the words that combine with the images to deliver the ad's message with impact. Art directors and copywriters have usually worked in teams, so the presentation of an idea could start with either words or pictures. Experienced art directors and copywriters develop the ability to cross disciplines and come up with rough words and images to convey their ideas, which they then hone with their partners. In successful teams, both copywriters and art directors come to appreciate each other's roles and talents.

In print ads, direct mail pieces, and catalogs, the length of the copy varies widely. But in almost all cases there are two copy elements: the headline and the body copy. A concise, memorable statement of the key selling message, the headline is paramount; in fact, it can be the only copy in an ad. Great headlines stand the test of time, as these do: from a 1892 Ivory soap ad, "99 and 44/100 percent pure"; from a 1912 ad for Morton Salt, "When it rains, it pours"; and from a vintage Rolls Royce ad, "At 60 miles per hour the only sound you hear is the ticking of the clock."

The headline should not be confused with another very important line that copywriters also craft, the tagline. This pithy, catchy statement is meant to be part of a brand's identity over time, often repeated after the changing body copy. Some noted taglines are: Maxwell House Coffee's "Good to the last drop"; Hallmark's "When you care enough to send the very best"; and Motel 6's "We'll leave a light on for you." Their familiarity is a good sign of their effectiveness.

Best

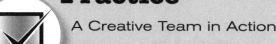

Practice

A Creative Team in Action

Coming up with a good creative idea is hard enough. Presenting it to the client convincingly and getting them to go along with it is a whole other task.

As an example of success on both counts, Sharon Ehrlich, senior copywriter, describes her work with partner Danny Rodriguez, senior art director, both at McCann Erickson, on a Wendy's "Smart Square" campaign in the "From the Front Lines" section of the Advertising Educational Foundation (http://www.aef.com). Here is a summary of Ehrlich's account:

"The idea came a lot quicker than selling it did," she writes, but even the idea had to be revised by the creative team. Focusing on Wendy's unusual square hamburgers, the team asked themselves where such hamburgers could come from. They hit upon a Square Cow, an independent type who "was proud not to follow the herd." Wary of offending people who didn't like "anthropomorphizing animals that are raised for food," Ehrlich and Rodriguez still held onto the idea of doing an animated campaign with a square as its hero. So they went with a "smart square living in a world of stupid circles; a simple metaphor that says square hamburgers are better than round hamburgers."

The first time they presented the idea to Wendy's, considered to be a traditional, conservative brand, they were relieved to get "a lot of laughs." The second time all but one person was sold, and on the third the sticking point was where the animated ads would run. "The fourth, fifth, sixth, and seventh time we presented," Ehrlich writes, "we couldn't believe we were still presenting it." At presentation number eight, "the client decided it wasn't the right time for Smart Square" and chose another campaign.

No wonder Ehrlich attributes Smart Square's eventual acceptance to sheer patience.

Smart Square "waited patiently in the corner" of the chief creative officer's office for about a year, when it came time to present new work to Wendy's and its newly hired chief marketing officer. "Wendy's loved it as much as they did the first time," Ehrlich concludes, "the only difference was, this time they bought it."

Thanks not only to patience, but persistence, too.

Like art directors, copywriters may start out at a junior level and progress to a senior role, and many creative directors were standout copywriters earlier in their careers.

Creative Director

When David Ogilvy was hiring creative directors at one point in his illustrious career, he advertised for "trumpeter swans." For good reason, as he explained: they "...must be capable of inspiring a motley crew of writers and artists; they must be sure-footed judges of campaigns for a wide range of different products; they must be good presenters; and they must have a colossal appetite for midnight oil."

This complex job is interpreted in so many different ways in the industry that a definition from an objective source like the Bureau of Labor Statistics is helpful. The creative director's main job is oversee the branding for clients to make sure that that the work done by the copywriters and art department reflects the needs of the client and the image the client wants to project. To do this the creative director helps to develop creative approaches and treatments that align with the client strategy.

As the arbiter of the quality of all creative work, the creative director stands to receive most of the credit for successful campaigns and awards, and the brunt of criticism when sales fall short or a client is displeased.

Although there are no set qualifications for the job, typically creative directors are former copywriters or art directors who were promoted to this top job. As department heads they are expected to be masters of their specialty and thoroughly understand the fine points of the complementary discipline. Due to the importance of television commercials, creative directors should have a good understanding of filmmaking and video production.

One challenging part of the creative director's job is managing their staff, as a team of creative people can present a very complex dynamic. To manage multiple teams the creative director must have a forceful personality and well-developed interpersonal skills. The job becomes even more daunting because of the fine line this leader must walk among staff with differing ideas, personalities, and agendas.

Another pitfall is that the politics of a large advertising agency and the necessity of pleasing clients can sometimes cause a creative director to lose the right to make the "final call" on his or her department's work.

Keeping
in Touch

The Changing Creative Team

The partnership between art director and copywriter is as well established in the world of work as the one between two cops on their beat or a comedian and his straight man. Although their end results may be clever and attention getting, the creative team's day-to-day work is hardly glamorous, as humorously described by Luke Sullivan in *Hey Whipple, Squeeze This*:

> So you try to get your pen moving. And you begin to work. And working, in this business, means staring at your partner's shoes.
>   That's what I've been doing from 9 to 5 for more than 20 years. Staring at the bottom of the disgusting tennis shoes on the feet of my partner, parked on the desk across from my disgusting tennis shoes. This is the sum and substance of life at an agency.

In recent years pondering duos like this have been undergoing changes at various agencies. For example, at Crispin Porter + Bogusky, there are still creative teams, but "ideas wind up coming in from all over the place," Alex Bogusky said in an interview posted in the Creatives section of Ihaveanidea.com. "The process at Crispin Porter + Bogusky is: everybody is 100 percent responsible for the quality of the work, all the time. So there's no hand-off. There's never this: 'Hey, we've got the insight. Here's the brief. Here you go.' That's why we have account people and strategic planners coming up with ideas too."

At Saatchi NY, executive creative director Tony Granger shook up creative hierarchies in the agency with a new floor plan. In his Creatives interview, he said he first brought all the creatives together on one floor, instead of having them spread out all over the agency's building. Then he set up a very large table and encouraged everyone to come out of their offices and work at it. "We have community areas where you can just hang out and do your thing, and we also have thinking rooms that the creatives can take over for a week, a month, two months, whatever," Granger says. "But most of the work is done around the big table.... It gives me the opportunity to have them collaborate more openly, and gives them the opportunity to see more work."

On the Cutting Edge

Research Trends

What trends will affect the work of advertising researchers in upcoming years? In *The Advertising Research Handbook*, Charles Young points out these:

An emergence of global research standards for global brands. As international companies build global brands with a unified message in all world markets, advertising campaigns will be increasingly visual in style. Prudent ad spending will be more dependent on a standard way to measure advertising performance from one region to another, and on the tools to identify how different cultural factors affect consumer response.

There will be more advertising measurement, not less. Given the increase in both expenses and media options for advertising, clients are insisting on more control over the process. In the name of accountability, they are challenging advertising agencies and research companies to provide more proof of value to justify ad budgets. So this important sector of advertising research will grow.

Most copy testing will move to the Internet. With the growing emphasis on speed of decision-making, the Internet is the obvious choice for shortening the time involved in the research step of creative development. Many suppliers have already begun migrating their advertising research to the Web for both television and print testing.

The new value proposition will be "filtering plus optimization," according to Young. Since the cost of producing ads will continue to

Successful creative directors in large agencies, where there can be several people with this title, can rise to the position of executive creative director or chief creative officer. And for a person in the top creative spot who can get a handle on the agency's finances and learn how to turn a profit, the company chairmanship becomes a distinct possibility.

Market Research Department

With the rise of account planning during the last decade, the role of advertising research has changed. Both planning and research go up, clients will want to broadcast only their strongest ideas and not spend a large portion of their budgets on average ones. To take advantage of this drive to make each ad work harder, research should validate the power of their diagnostics, proving they can help make ads more effective.

Ad research will put a new emphasis on "holistic" or 360-degree measurement of integrated advertising campaigns. Both globalization and new rich, multi-sensory media will continue to challenge researchers to think beyond the boundaries of language and semantics in understanding how advertising builds brand image.

New heuristic models will help managers make ad decisions by clarifying confusing media fragmentation. These new models will describe how different media work; for instance, the use of television versus print. With these new tools, advertising managers will have a common measurement framework with which to compare the relative advantages of advertising on television, in print, or on the Internet.

Calculations of advertising's return on investment will begin to incorporate measures of creative quality. Without measuring creative quality, current media-mix models are biased toward the volume of audience or ad spend. In the future, sophisticated modelers will start to include a "quality" variable in these models, particularly as new forms of tracking research begin to provide relative performance rankings of competitive ads.

attempt to understand consumers' motivation, behavior, and reactions to products and the ways of advertising them. While account planning has initiated new ways of eliciting and analyzing qualitative information, agency's research departments have focused on quantitative results. These two contrasting approaches to research within the industry, and sometimes within the same agency, have understandably led to some tension.

Yet there is a need for both approaches, according to one of the main proponents of account planning, Jon Steel. In his book *Truth, Lies & Advertising* he writes that "...like every other source of information available to advertisers, quantitative research and the numbers it yields should not always be taken at face value. Numbers, just like focus group respondents, are capable of misleading, and even lying, and always require a commonsense filter before they can be used with confidence."

Quantitative research can be either customized for a specific client or syndicated, that is, the results of a single research study applied to a number of companies. Researchers can study the performance of ads in any single medium or of a complete, integrated, multi-media campaign, including online ads. For television commercials, researchers employ pretesting, also known as copy testing, to predict in-market performance of an ad before it airs. Pre-testing is also used to identify weak spots within an ad to improve performance, to edit it for shorter running times, and to select images from the spot to use in an integrated campaign's print ad.

Post-testing, or ad tracking, provides in-market research monitoring a brand's performance, including brand awareness, brand preference, product usage, and attitudes. Researchers conduct tracking by interviewing consumers by telephone or online.

Media Department

Media Buyer and Media Planner
The media department of an agency determines how to use a client's budget most efficiently so the advertising reaches the right audience at the right times for optimal effect. The main roles in this area of the business are the media buyer and the media planner. In the previous century, these two positions were very similar. Today, though the media buyer still performs the traditional function of negotiating with various media representatives on rates, placement, deadline, and other matters, the media planner's role has changed markedly. In some agencies, even the job title has changed to alternatives like communications planner, brand planner, or strategist.

The planner's job description and title have been revised, not surprisingly, because of all the new developments in media. Besides the standard media such as television, radio, print, and outdoor, to formulate an integrated strategy the planner now has to consider digital media, in-store promotions, product placement, public relations, and other emerging channels. Another change in this profession is that in addition to planning departments within advertising agencies, there are now a number of stand-alone, global planning agencies.

As media opportunities grow increasingly fragmented, advertisers now look for specialization among these planning agencies.

Planners commonly consider media according to three categories: above the line (ATL), below the line (BTL), and through the line (TTL). "The line" derives from a now defunct accounting practice by which profitable services were recorded "above the line."

In general, ATL media are conventional television, radio, print, and online banners. BTL uses more direct methods to promote products and services, including direct mail, e-mail, public relations, and sales promotions for which a fee is agreed upon and charged up front. TTL refers to a combination of above- and below-the-line strategies. For example, an ATL commercial prompts the audience to come into a certain store. When they go to the store, they are presented with BTL promotions like coupons or contest-entry forms.

New Business or Business Development Department

The positions are called new business manager, coordinator of new business, director of new business, and other titles. But basically, they are all rainmakers—the people who bring in new clients to the agency.

This is an essential function in many industries, and the new business staff in an agency performs some of the same tasks as their counterparts in other lines of work. They research markets to find opportunities, generate leads, mail solicitations to potential clients, meet with prospects and pitch them, set up a database for all prospecting activity, and respond to requests for proposals (RFPs). One element of attracting new business that is more important to the advertising industry than to most others is the pitch—a formal presentation of campaign ideas to the client that is given in competition with a few "finalist" agencies vying for the same business.

To increase an agency's chances of winning a new account fairly, the American Association of Advertising Agencies (AAAA) has compiled a list of guidelines for a pitch, which are summarized in these points:

1. Since compensation can be the determinant in selecting the winning agency, discussing fees early in negotiations can help you focus prospecting on accounts that are "on the same page."

Problem
Solving

Red Cross Responds to Storms

This example of a quickly executed, successful ad campaign is an edited version of an article in the "Case Study" section of the Advertising Educational Foundation Web site (http://www.aef.com).

The Problem

During their busiest times many ad agencies might feel like a storm has hit them. But when an actual storm, Hurricane Charley, slammed into the western coast of Florida in August 2004, only to be followed by four other hurricanes during the following seven weeks, American Red Cross Advertising Unit faced an unprecedented crisis. Just one week before Hurricane Charley made landfall, the American Red Cross's Disaster Relief Fund (DRF) was at an all-time low. This balance fell far short of what the Red Cross would need to respond to the problems caused by the hurricanes.

The organization's public relations staff had to act quickly to launch initiatives that would help build trust in the organization and inspire people to donate money to the Red Cross. Advertising was a key component of this response, communicating the urgent need for people to support the massive disaster relief efforts of the American Red Cross.

The Advertising Strategy

The Advertising Unit created new public service announcements (PSAs) to appeal to the public's interest in disaster relief and in the Red Cross response to the hurricane, and to encourage financial donations.

Two new 30-second television PSAs and four coordinating radio PSAs were created in-house, saving the organization thousands of dollars in outside costs. These spots took an emotional approach, featuring Johnny Cash's rendition of "Bridge Over Troubled Water." The television ads showed a montage of black-and-white photos of disasters' impact.

American Red Cross president and CEO Marsha Evans appeared in a television appeal. A previously used print ad featuring Ms. Evans was repurposed for use as a disaster-relief appeal directed to military audiences, maximizing available resources.

Various print PSAs, in English and Spanish, were created to encourage continued support for the American Red Cross hurricane relief effort, especially as time passed and the media covered other stories.

Actress and American Red Cross Celebrity Cabinet member Christina Sanchez donated her time to record five disaster-relief radio PSAs in Spanish.

The 2004 hurricane season also marked the first time that the Red Cross comprehensively used online search engine advertising.

Advertising Placement

In the days leading up to each of the four hurricanes, the Advertising Unit encouraged the media to use the relief advertising in the aftermath of the disasters. These efforts brought significant PSA placements in the initial days following each hurricane. The continued support from national newspapers and magazines, television, cable and radio networks, and other organizations was critical to inspiring the public and corporate donors to contribute throughout the devastating hurricane season.

Results

By the end of September 2004, the American Red Cross had received $1,119,053 in donated advertising from television, radio, and print media. By November 2004, approximately 85,000 visitors had been directed to the American Red Cross Disaster Relief Fund Web page as a result of online search engine advertising. Having communicated its critical message to the public, the American Red Cross raised funds that supported a massive relief effort, which opened more than 1,800 shelters, housed more than 425,000 people, and served about eleven million meals and snacks to disaster victims.

2. Potential conflicts of interest should be cleared up early.
3. Prospects will most likely request speculative strategic thinking and creative executions. The amount of work provided should be proportionate to the potential value and likely conversion of the prospective account. If speculative creative work is requested, it should be as finished as the work that's presented in an ongoing agency-client relationship.
4. Agencies should value the creative work that's part of their pitch. They should charge market rates for it, or if that is a problem, consider retaining copyrights. Some clients think token payments for creative work that's presented mean they own it. This practice is unrewarding for the agency and in general bad for business.
5. "Pay for play is odious." It is simply wrong to have to pay to participate in a new business pitch, either directly or indirectly.
6. Agencies should provide prospects (and their consultants) only the information they are comfortable sharing. Sharing confidential information should be avoided, even when told that similar data is normally shared with marketers and their representatives. For instance, the Association of National Advertisers, Inc., and the AAAA agree that it is always inappropriate to share individual salary information with prospects, clients, or consultants. Although prospects and consultants sometimes ask for other clients' financial information, sharing it could be construed as a breach of client confidentiality.
7. Agencies should be confident of the value of their services, especially during fee negotiations. If they truly believe that they can help build the prospect's business, they should charge accordingly. Many in the business say agencies that undercharge their competitors solely to get business are working specifically against their own interests and more generally against the interests of the advertising business as a whole.
8. Anyone in an agency who has anything to do with setting or updating fee amounts should be trained in negotiation skills.

Print and Production Department

The job descriptions are compiled from those posted by the American Association of Advertising Agencies (http://www.aaaa.org).

Art Buyer

Found primarily in large agencies, this specialized position procures the photography, illustrations, and other artwork used in ads. This may include obtaining the rights to reproduce fine art owned by museums or private sources. Working with the creative director to maintain an agency's aesthetic and quality standards, the art buyer recommends photographers and artists who can deliver good work that meets the schedule and budget.

A large part of the art buyer's time is spent negotiating cost and timing with artists' representatives, coordinating art purchases with preproduction, and preparing for the reproduction of images in print media. Like so many other agency staff, the buyer must also obtain client approval, in this case for the artworks and photo-shoot details.

Print Buyer

More than simply buying vendors' services, this position's main responsibility is controlling the quality of all print work. Accomplishing this involves identifying state-of-the-art vendors, conducting vendor bidding and selection, getting estimates for printed jobs, and purchasing them. The print buyer sets timetables for all print work and works with the traffic manager to ensure that the timetable is followed. Sometimes this print expert advises art directors on how their designs can best be produced in print.

Print Director

As the head of the print department, the director manages the staff and their work in print production, traffic, and forwarding (or binding of print pieces), and coordinates these activities with creative, account services, media, and accounting. Reporting to the chief creative officer, this director must establish standards for print operation and quality of work. On a day-to-day basis, the job also involves informing accounting of job orders, production estimates, supplier bills, completed or canceled jobs, and more.

Print Producer

The producer focuses specifically on the pre-press aspects of the printing process, starting with a review of electronic specs for disk preparation with a separator or printer, and the purchase of all

Best
Practice

Award-winning Media Plans

No matter how various media are labeled, the real skill in planning is how to select the best combination of them for a client's advertising. To recognize agencies that have done this effectively, Adweek.com presents Media Plan Awards; here are a few of the 2008 winners:

Timberland campaign by MediaHub at Mullen, part of IPG–The boot-maker Timberland has long been aware of the environmental impact of producing their products. In the same spirit, their media planners launched a marketing plan in the Boston test market for the new Earthkeepers boot, which was designed to leave a small carbon footprint. They arranged to measure the energy required to power TV, radio, and Web ad executions. Carbon dioxide emissions associated with the campaign were then offset with wind power generated by the Jiminy Peak Mountain Resort in western Massachusetts. The plan incorporated earth-conscious elements throughout, right down to soy-based inks for the print ads. Breaking with dependency on electric radios, Timberland ran fewer promos on this media than usual, limiting them to only when rain or heavy winds were in the forecast; that way they were able to reduce their advertising's carbon footprint while still selling a profitable amount of boots. And ads on buses and subways encouraged riders to keep up their energy-saving ways.

Reebok campaign by Aegis Media North America/Carat–For Reebok's "Run Easy" campaign, out-of-home and Internet ad buys made up most of the nearly $18 million budget. Focused on the benefits of moderate running as opposed to grueling training for

separations, retouching, and printing. Before artwork is bought, the producer makes sure it is prepped to look as creative intends when it is printed. This position also reviews all proofs with art directors in order to understand their revisions, and works with the supplier to determine the best method for executing them. Another important function is supervising film preparation.

Work with other departments of the agency includes preparing preproduction timetables and providing them to the traffic manager, and notifying accounts of any pre-press estimate overages.

long, competitive races, the campaign made use of localized signage: In San Francisco, signs read, "These hills will chew you up and spit you out. Run Easy." Utilizing new media, other posters encouraged consumers to text message the company describing what scenery they came across or what music they listened to while running. Those who did got a reply directing them to a Reebok site, which enabled users to create jogging routes using Google Maps. The media planners struck a deal with the photo-sharing site Flickr that let users upload photos of scenes along their routes and post their favorite exercise tunes. Via the site, they also could form groups to compare notes with others about running techniques. Carat also set up profiles on social networks like Facebook, which alone attracted 14,000 friends.

VW Jetta campaign by Crispin Porter + Bogusky, MediaCom—The planners at MediaCom wanted to capitalize on the Jetta's safety, which had been recognized with the prestigious four-star front-impact rating from the National Highway Traffic Safety Administration. Working with creative partners Crispin Porter + Bogusky, they placed a conventional billboard depicting the life-sized front end of a Jetta, along with the symbolic four gold stars, in the right field of several major league baseball stadiums. When a baseball player collided with the ad as he ran after a fly ball, making the old-fashioned type of billboard interactive, it provided a clever demonstration of safety. The ad's placement captured the attention not only of fans in the stands but also of sports photographers, netting VW an estimated $4 million worth of free exposure on air, on the Web, and in print, delivering 290 million total impressions.

Talent Department

All areas of an advertising agency aim to find and keep talent. But the talent department works with talent in a different sense, namely the payment of the performers in television and radio commercials produced by the agency. They manage these costs in conjunction with account management, creative, and traffic.

The talent department has to be well versed in the union codes and contract codes of such industry groups as the Screen Actors

Guild (SAG), the American Federation of Television and Radio Artists (AFTRA), and the American Federation of Musicians (AFM). Talent staff works with the legal department on specific contracts for sports figures and celebrities. They also maintain records of all commercials, including year of production, expiration dates, periods of first fixed cycles, and holding fees. Outside the agency the talent staff must understand commercial producers' specific requirements and negotiate with talent agents.

Job titles in this department include director of talent payments, broadcast talent payment manager, and talent payment coordinator.

Traffic Manager–Broadcast

The liaison between the agency and broadcast networks and stations, the traffic manager schedules and sends commercial materials and pertinent instructions to these media.

Inside the agency the broadcast traffic manager maintains the commercial schedule and the inventory of production assets.

Traffic Manager–Print

Given all the print jobs at various stages that can be circulating through an agency at the same time, someone in this position could feel like a traffic cop. But unlike the police, the traffic manager documents the progress of each job and often has to speed it up.

After receiving a print ad from account services, the traffic manager consults with creative to set deadlines for each stage of job completion and then follows up (some creatives might say "hounds") to see that that these dates are met. This manager reports to all concerned on the status of the jobs, and expedites "rush" jobs. Another important responsibility of this position is obtaining approvals of art, mechanicals, and proofs from inside the agency and, through the account executive, the client. The final stage in traffic is making sure finished materials (insertions) are shipped to publications on time.

Public Relations

Agency versus Corporation

Public relations professionals practice either in an agency or as part of a corporation large enough to have its own PR department. Although they perform similar functions in both environments, there are different titles and specific tasks within each of them, according to

Careers in Public Relations: A Guide to Opportunities in a Dynamic Industry, from the Council of Public Relations Firms (http://www.prfirms. org/_data/n_0001/resources/live/career_guide.pdf).

The entry-level position in an agency is called an account coordinator, while the counterpart in a corporation is known as a PR coordinator. The account coordinator assists the agency's account executive with maintaining close client relations, writing press releases, planning publicity events, tracking trends to identify opportunities for media coverage, and following up on press releases. PR coordinators help corporate PR specialists arrange press conferences, write speeches and opinion pieces for the company CEO, prepare annual reports, and submit products for awards.

Within an agency, account executives can tailor their careers to become generalists or focus on a specific industry. Generalists work with all stakeholders, acquire knowledge of every type of media, carry out a variety of communications and research assignments, and gain firsthand information about a full range of industries. All this experience helps the generalist hone in on his special talents and interests in new jobs. Specialists become authorities in a single industry, knowing personally its opinion makers, analysts, bloggers, and the media professionals covering it.

After performing their jobs successfully for several years, account executives may be promoted to an account supervisor, with full responsibility for the relationship with a client, leading the account staff, providing services, directing the work of other U.S. and international offices supporting the client, and managing the P&L (profit and loss) of the account.

Accomplished account supervisors often take on more responsibilities as a group director of accounts, often dedicated to a specific industry. A group director balances staff time among several clients, gains knowledge of group clients' industries, and recruits new business for the group.

In the next level of PR agency management there are two types of positions. Practice directors help their firms stake out a claim for a particular industry or service. As the experts in this specialty, practice directors guide research, build databases, share knowledge among branch offices, solicit new business, and train staff. General managers head up an agency's operations in a particular city or region. Partnering with practice directors, they lead business development and manage the staff and administration, thus generating revenue and managing costs, both keys to the bottom line.

Problem
....▶
Solving

LEGO® Builders of Tomorrow Campaign

This is a summary of a case study posted on the Council of Public Relations Firms Web site (http://www.prfirms.org):

In 2006, LEGO enlisted the Boston agency 360 PR to help reestablish the iconic plastic brick as a leading children's entertainment brand with parents of children who already use new media and have little time for unstructured play. The agency created LEGO Builders of Tomorrow, a platform from which to talk to parents about the importance of fostering creative play to benefit children immediately and as creative adults. The campaign communicated with parents directly, providing them with online tools created by 360 PR to help foster creative play. This was accomplished through a variety of online tools that 360 PR recommended, including:

- A Web site for parents, http://www.legobuildersoftomorrow. com, to deliver practical play tips and inspirational stories from parents
- A podcast series, called LEGO Playtime Podcasts
- A blog by a dad very familiar with LEGOs

Objectives

The objective was to "begin a dialogue with parents about the importance of imaginative play," and to position LEGO as a resource to help parents foster it.

LEGO research had shown that younger, Generation Y moms, responsible for making most of the family's toy-buying decisions, grew up with many play options and have no strong connection with the LEGO brand. So when they shop for toys, LEGO is not "top of mind." These moms are also increasingly turning to the Internet as a source of parenting information.

In addition, 360 PR commissioned a survey that found today's dads are more actively involved on the home front, including playtime, than in prior generations. The survey also found that LEGO was the dads' favorite toy when they were growing up. So LEGO created a blog that was authored by a dad who was enthusiastic about the building blocks.

Research

Besides the research showing that an increasing number of parents were turning to the Internet for advice about child-rearing, a 2006 study by the Kaiser Family Foundation found that children were spending more time with passive, electronic media, leaving less time for hands-on play like LEGO building.

Also, 360 PR commissioned new research on what toys parents wanted to give their children at the holidays and have them play with all year, and on dads' involvement in playtime in the home. The agency also conducted interviews with child-development experts via the Web site Momstown.com.

Tactics

In addition to several traditional media components, 360 PR created the Builders of Tomorrow Web site as a central source for playtime information. They assembled a panel of child-development experts, educators, and parents to provide compelling, useful content for the site. And LEGO Playtime Podcasts, scripted and produced by the agency, kept the site fresh and provided tips for on-the-go parents.

To drive traffic to the site, 360 PR publicized the URL with the media and highlighted it in 10,000 brochures distributed to parents at LEGO store events in six markets.

Execution

In addition to the content already noted, The Builders of Tomorrow Web site featured:

- Stories of high-profile LEGO fans, like the founders of Google, clothing designer/mom Eileen Fisher, and actor/dad Matthew Broderick attributing part of their success to having time for imaginative play as children.
- Details about a LEGO brick donation program to benefit schools in New Orleans for children affected by Hurricane Katrina. The company matched every donated LEGO brick with a new one.

(continues on next page)

Problem

Solving

(continued from previous page)

- A Scholarship Contest for kids making a difference by "building" their communities. Winners' stories were featured on the Web site.

Results

The Builders of Tomorrow Web site has been featured in dozens of media outlets, including national parenting, kids, and classroom publications; newspapers and magazines; other Web sites; and audio releases. The total circulation of media that featured the Web site is over 46 million, translating to over 92 million impressions with pass along. Six months after launch, the site was attracting more than 5,000 unique monthly visitors, with more than 17,000 pages viewed.

Standout directors and managers may attain the title of an agency vice president, who helps manage the firm, meets with high-level clients, sets overall strategy, comes up with new services for existing clients, and pitches to prospects.

In most other businesses the only way a vice president can advance in the agency is to become the president or CEO. But in public relations, VPs can also become senior counselors, who work on major assignments like advising a large corporation on the acquisition of a company in another country.

Practice Groups

Within an agency, PR practitioners often specialize in working with certain types of industries, forming what is called practice groups. Here are summaries of the main groups' work, described in greater detail on the Public Relations Society of America's Web site (http://www.prsa.org):

Cause-related marketing (CRM)—Strategic combination of corporate or product marketing and philanthropy. For example, in a transaction-based CRM program, every time a product or service is purchased a small donation is made to a nonprofit partner, providing contributions and visibility to the cause and enhancing the company's reputation with its consumers.

Community relations—Building support among citizens and groups where an organization is based.

Consumer marketing—Determines and communicates a brand's value to engage consumers, trade partners, the media, business decision makers, and opinion leaders. Can be used to launch a brand, reposition it, or maintain awareness of it.

Crisis communications/preparedness planning—Raises issues that could become a crisis for clients and then organizes a response strategy—materials and messages that the client will need to handle the most likely situations. Involves simulation training to confront senior executives with crisis vulnerability and risks, and to help them make decisions in a simulated crisis environment. Usually leads to steps that can be taken to avoid potential problems.

Employee relations—Communicates with an organization's employees to build morale, enhance job retention, and recruit new employees.

Financial relations—Responds to and communicates with the organization's shareholders and the investment community.

Government relations—Informs legislatures and government agencies on behalf of an organization or corporation. Provides information on which policies and decisions will be based.

Health care—Works with health-care related clients such as pharmaceutical or insurance companies, hospitals, and health care providers. Builds awareness of specific products or illnesses. Enlists researchers and third-party supporters such as doctors and university affiliates to support campaigns.

Industry analyst/trade relations—Responds to and communicates with firms and analysts within the industry of the client.

Issues management—Monitors opinions and trends regarding markets and other matters. Stays abreast of public policy related to an organization.

Organizational communications—Aligns management, human resources, and IT systems to motivate employees and share knowledge across the organization.

Public affairs—Stays in contact with governments and groups who help determine public policies and legislation.

Public Relations Supporting Services

The following are additional services that some agencies provide to their clients, again distilled from the Public Relations Society of America (http://www.prsa.org):

Graphic design—Provides logos, PowerPoint presentations, press kit folders, letterhead, and business cards.

Market intelligence—Informs management on trends, emerging public attitudes, and the impact of public opinion.

Measurement and evaluation—Critical to understanding the value and effectiveness of PR activities or programs. Involves research techniques that measure both PR program outputs ("How many people read a specific article or heard a specific message?") and outcomes ("How did the program influence or change people's behaviors?").

Research—Determines opinions and attitudes about a client, its competitors, marketplace, customers, and the media through surveys and analysis of source material and data.

Chapter 4

Tips for Success

It may be on a computer file or a CD instead of in the traditional black bag, but a portfolio showcasing ads is still crucial for any creative in the business. How crucial? In their book *Pick Me: Breaking Into Advertising and Staying There*, Nancy Vonk and Janet Kestin tell beginners the question is not whether a degree or a portfolio is more important, it is "All your worldly goods or your portfolio?" They also give a hint on how difficult the preparation of a portfolio, or "book," as it is known in the industry, can be by titling the chapter on this subject "Portfolio Preparation: Like Giving Birth, Only More Painful."

Fortunately, Vonk and Kestin, who are both creative directors, also offer some good advice on putting together the kind of book that impresses creative directors (CDs) and generates job offers.

The most important criteria for whether or not to include a particular ad in your book, they say, is that the work be "outstanding." This rule of thumb applies to how many samples to include (they would rather see four great ads than 10 average ones but encourage adding more work later), whether to include spec or "unproduced" work, and a multimedia campaign versus a single work.

Vonk and Kestin are more interested in the quality of ideas than in the type of products that are in the ad ("even dog food" is OK). For beginner creatives they suggest not working up comp ads for famous brands like Nike, because less experienced people will have a hard time living up to the outstanding work already done for these products. These creative directors also advise against including scripts in a portfolio.

On a practical level, there is no need to make multiple copies of a complete, costly portfolio, according to the authors. A job candidate can leave behind some black-and-white copies of the best samples instead. It is not uncommon to get conflicting opinions on creative work, they add, so keep showing it, weigh the responses, and "use your gut" to determine the true value of the work. A portfolio will always be a work in progress, Vonk and Kestin say, to be revised and improved throughout an advertising career. To someone who wrote to them about never feeling satisfied with her book, the authors replied, "Welcome to advertising."

One of the co-creative directors' sources in *Pick Me*, Bob Barrie, a veteran art director at Fallon/Minneapolis, has a practical approach to evaluating a portfolio. When he looks at young creatives' books, he tries "to imagine their work thrown into the real world. If it seems like it might survive, or at least dog-paddle for a while with its head above water, I am always impressed."

In an article on Ihaveanidea.org, "Glad Tidings for the Young and Terrified," Suzanne Pope writes: "The best portfolios are an ever-changing snapshot of their owners' evolving abilities; a stagnant book suggests stagnant talent." What is more, she says, "Taste in advertising is...a moving target, much like fashion." So although visual ads were all the rage some years ago, "To show a book with no copy today is like showing up for a first date wearing shoulder pads and Flock of Seagulls hair."

So to keep a portfolio fresh, Pope recommends that both copy-writers and art directors looking for jobs write five ads every day about any product or service, real or made up. Then those ads should be filed away and not looked at for some time. "The point of the exercise is to open your creative sluices and to get you away from regarding any one ad as precious or sacrosanct," she points out. "Never will a creative director view even your best ad as the Magna Carta, and you shouldn't either."

Another contributor to Ihaveanidea.org, Ronnie Lebow, also offers some tips on portfolios in his article "Pounding the Creative Pavement," including:

> Just because someone did not like your book doesn't mean the next person you see will not love it. It is art. Everyone has an opinion.
>
> Do not come across as a jack-of all trades. If you want to do print ads, show a book full of your best print ads. Do not go to an agency that does outdoor with a book full of direct mail.

Best
Practice

Speakers Advance Careers

Showcasing your expertise as a speaker at a trade show, conference, or other professional meeting can generate interest and even new business leads for your company, and demonstrates your value and credibility in your profession. Susan Bratton tells ad and PR professionals about landing "speak ops" in "How to Successfully Pitch Yourself as a Speaker," an article posted on TalentZoo.com (http://www.talentzoo.com).

Bratton writes that after doing the basics of selecting a conference where your expertise applies, determining who is programming the sessions, and who the attendees will be, you should:

Give your speech an angle that will help differentiate this conference from its competitors and attract its target audience. This is the most important part of successful pitching.

Make sure your submission is not self-serving but is instead balanced, objective, and something difficult to find online or in a publication. Beyond facts it should include "experiential learning, tips, tricks, wisdom, analysis, examples, market overviews, etc." Even better, Bratton says programmers find "primary research that's exclusive to that conference...nearly irresistible."

Submit a complete abstract that includes a suggested session title, what attendees will learn, and other speakers who might add to a discussion of this subject, including their name, title, company affiliation, and contact information.

"The submissions that list other authorities are more likely to be chosen than those that just pitch a single person." You are doing a little work for the conference chair, and showing you are a specialist in this area by having a national or global perspective.

If you are not selected, ask why so that you can learn from your submission and make future ones stronger.

Now that you know the best way to apply for a speak op, research all the events at which you would like to speak. Create a spreadsheet that lists all the events, their schedule, their conference chair or programming decision-maker, and deadlines for submission. (Shows generally are organized and the agendas completed about six months ahead of time so they can be marketed.) Working backward, apply to each show.

Buy tickets to award shows. You can corner and network with everyone who did not return any of your calls, and they usually feel guilty about it.

Jumping Beyond Junior

It has been said that the toughest job in advertising is landing that first job in the business. But Brian Sheppard, a senior writer at Ogilvy & Mather, disagrees: He thinks it is even tougher to get beyond the "junior" level at which art directors and copywriters spend their first few years in the business. Having gone through that rite of passage himself a few years ago, Sheppard has written an article for Ihaveanidea.org intended to help creatives who are now juniors to follow in his footsteps. Here are his main suggestions and summaries of his reasoning:

- Do not be intimidated. You may be in an agency "where you're surrounded by people whose names you've read in award show books." But do not forget that "all those seasoned creatives started as juniors, and they all still float lots of crappy ideas." Sheppard says he has known more than one senior writer or art director who is threatened by "that bright and shiny hip kid down the hall. So it cuts both ways."

- Be indispensable. "Weasel your way into every job possible during your first year," Sheppard writes. "Help out on every pitch, spec project or pro bono job your office is doing. Make it so that the people you work for actually believe that they'd be much worse off if you weren't there."

- Work with everybody. "Try and get involved in jobs with every senior team in the department. You'll be really visible, and you'll learn a ton," Sheppard suggests. "Try and work with all the different account teams —you'll soak up more about your clients' businesses from them than anyone."

- Do not be difficult. Sheppard says he has known a number of coworkers who have met this description. "None of them lasted. Not one. No amount of talent can justify being a mouthy, know-it-all, pain in the ass."

- Get close to your creative director. Sheppard thinks that since the CD hired you, you are entitled to some mentoring from him or her. This is "the single most important person in determining the direction of your work and your career."

To get to know the CD, "Show up unannounced at their (office) door... Talk about the movie you just saw, or how a job is going." Once you've established a good relationship with your CD, he writes, "the more jobs will flow your way" and the easier it will be to present work to him or her.

- "Present like a madman." To develop strong presentation skills, Sheppard advises, "ask to go to presentations of work that you weren't part of, so you can see how the senior guys sell their ads. If you can learn to present like a pro, you'll sell way more work and you'll appear 10 times as mature. It's the best way to gain cred with your CD, your account team, and your clients."

In sum, Sheppard thinks that for juniors to get to the next level of intermediate, "You've got to change the way the people perceive you, and that is tough." How should they perceive you? He says that "you want to be seen as more than just having potential...that potential has to actually be coming through in your projects."

Juniors receive a more seasoned perspective on getting ahead from 13 very successful art directors and copywriters profiled in *How to Succeed in Advertising When All You Have Is Talent*, by Laurence Minsky and Emily Tornton Calvo. Several of these veterans, many of whom have been in the business since before today's juniors were born, agree on these key points:

- Be likeable. Amil Gargano, founding partner of the agency Amil Gargano and Partners, echoes the words of several colleagues when he says, "I think personality is as important as the work presented...I've made the mistake of hiring some people who had great portfolios, but were arrogant people...I want to be around people who enjoy producing everything from a commercial to a matchbook cover."

- Find a good creative partner to work with. "You need somebody who listens and someone whose ideas are worth listening to," says Don Easdon, founding partner of Heater/Easdon. Mike Koelker, a director of creative development for Foote Cone & Belding/USA, tells junior copywriters and art directors, "As early as you can, team up and start building a portfolio...Even if you're not interviewing as a team, you can talk about the working relationship. The creative director will realize you have an idea of what the business is all about."

- Study the annuals. These are books of the year's award-winning ads, like the One Shows, New York Art Director Annuals and Communications Arts Advertising Annuals. "Start to understand why some of these ads are really special," says Tom McElligott, cofounder of Fallon McElligott. "You're getting a glimpse into the minds of some very good creative advertising people. You have to start somewhere. Even Picasso was influenced by other painters." Stan Richards, Founder of the Richards Group, recommends reading the annuals because in the popular weekly magazines the "ads are 90 percent garbage...you won't ever develop a sense for really terrific work (from them). Emulate the best work...."

- Show "hunger" and "enthusiasm." Products may become less or more popular and styles of advertising go in and out of fashion, but these words to the wise seem always to apply to jobseekers, and in many industries. "If there were five people interviewing for a position and they all had great art direction and great ideas, the one that would get it is the one who showed the desire," according to Nancy Rice, a group creative director at the former DDB Needham/Chicago and the cofounder of two ad agencies. Ted Bell, a former president and chief creative officer at Leo Burnett/USA, agrees: "If you really have a passion for the business, that comes across and helps you...People sense you're going to have a certain energy about you. Or you're not. And who would you rather have working for you? The guy who loves the work."

Selling Your Own Brand Online

In almost all professions, using social media is becoming an increasingly popular way of looking for that next career move. People in advertising and PR, who are most likely already using these media to promote their clients' products, should have an advantage in maximizing this approach for job searching. Think of utilizing social media as part of an ongoing, multimedia campaign for your own personal brand—a campaign that also includes your résumé, your portfolio, and that old standby, word of mouth (or, to bring it up to date, networking).

In her March 28, 2009 article in the *New York Times*, "Putting Yourself Out There on a Shelf to Buy," Alina Tugend writes that though she does not "embrace it wholeheartedly," personal online branding is necessary to control what potential employers will find when they search your name. And it is essential that they do find you, Tugend says, since "Not being online today is akin to not existing."

Tugend recommends starting with the basics by establishing your brand on LinkedIn, Facebook, or Twitter. These sites also have helpful features like Twitter's job search (http://www.twitterjobsearch. com) and JobAngels (http://www.twitter.com/jobangels), an online mentoring match-up. Then Tugend suggests joining a few sites related to your field.

The next step is trickier: figuring out your unique brand or niche, or as Tugend describes it, "what makes you you and not that other Brand You over there." She summarizes a four-step process proposed by Dan Schawbel, author of *Me 2.0: Build a Powerful Brand to Achieve Career Success*:

1. Discover your passion and combine it with your experience.
2. Assemble a "personal branding tool kit" with things like your résumé, online profile, and blog, all consistently portraying your brand.
3. Pitch your brand.
4. Monitor online conversations about brand; use Google Alerts to be notified every time your name comes up.

As an example of consistency, Schawbel maintains his brand by using "Personal Branding—Dan Schawbel" wherever he appears online, Tugend points out, ensuring that "whether the topic or the person is searched, he will come up prominently."

Then it is time to build an online community. Tugend quotes Veronica Fielding, president of Digital Brand Expressions: "You want to find groups—alumni, former employees of your last jobs, trade groups." Join the groups and follow the online discussions; when you feel you have something to contribute, post your opinion. By branding yourself as someone knowledgeable in a certain field, Fielding says, you will come to mind when someone is filling a job in that area.

A personal brand should not only be unique but authentic. To help define a brand that meets these criteria, Tugend quotes Sherry

Best
Practice

Building Customer Relations with Words

In online advertising, building a long-term, one-to-one relationship with customers is said to be key for sales.

Yet this relationship can't be built with customer data alone, according to Nick Usborne in his book *Net Words: Creating High-Impact Online Copy.* Instead, copywriters should use research data to learn how to talk to customers in a way that will build the relationship.

Some of Usborne's recommendations are:

- Think about the tone of the copy and the company image it projects. Phrases like "we endeavor to become a leading contributor" and "corporate citizenship focuses on who we are" sound aloof and cold. Customers will more readily connect with the company through "Simpler language. Simpler concepts. Simpler promises."
- Practice "permissive marketing" by recognizing that the Web is a "shared space where the voices of the customers are as loud as those of the marketers." So the tone of a site's messaging should be inclusive and friendly.
- "Match the language to the moment." After initial contact with a customer and the start of the relationship, a more informal tone can be used.
- Allay customer anxiety about using this relatively new media with reassuring language and a straightforward privacy statement.
- Update site copy regularly to ensure its consistency with e-mails and other customer contacts.
- "Good writing can't save a bad relationship." Customer experiences have to live up to the promises made in copy. As Usborne puts it: "An imperfect policy stated honestly will do more good for your business than the same policy" described to sound better than it is.

Beck Paprocki, author of *The Complete Idiot's Guide to Branding Yourself,* who suggests thinking about three things you are good at, three things you are passionate about, and three things other people think you are good at. Ideally, you will have a personal profile before an actual job search begins, so you will be already part of a network.

Blogs and personal Web sites are other ways to promote "Brand You," but they must be focused and updated. A boring blog or an unprofessional Web site is worse than none at all, according to Paprocki.

Double Duty in Ad Disciplines

One key to satisfaction and ultimately to success in advertising is finding what area of the business—creative, accounts, media, etc.— is best suited to your talents. Yet some ad professionals take an available job in one department only to find that their true calling is in another. Lonelle Selbo recalls how she resolved such a conflict in an article on Ihaveanidea.org, titled "Moonlighting: How to be a Successful Suit and a Brilliant Creative on the Sly."

Intending to work in "the greatest industry in the world, as a top writer," after a five-month's search Selbo found herself as the account manager (the one and only) in a small agency. She uses her flair for writing to describe what it takes to be an account executive: "The world over, there is no more demanding a job than that of an advertising account executive. To be successful in this field requires the discipline of a kamikaze pilot, the sincerity of an evangelist, the versatility of a chameleon and the ability to seamlessly meld all these characteristics into one, clean-cut, cucumber-cool package."

Selbo rose to the occasion and got through her months-long learning period "with few mishaps and even the occasional accolade." But since she was not doing creative writing, she felt "unfulfilled." Until one breakthrough day: "I was researching a client's product, dreaming up concepts for my own private pleasure, when suddenly the solution became obvious." Instead of outsourcing ads to freelance copywriters, Selbo, "who knew the client's business" and "had researched and devised their strategies," could also write the ads and save the agency some money.

Yet she soon found out that being a client's all-service, one-person team has its downside: "Ultimately, you are responsible for the prep, the action, the inspection, the revision, and the presentation." Account executives routinely make concessions to clients when presenting their creative team's work, but in Selbo's case she was compromising something she herself had "given birth to." The split between "Creative You" and "Suit You" made it seem like "Every day you wage war on yourself...."

But as an indication of what some ad pros will endure to do the job they really love, Selbo found her double duty "infinitely rewarding.

At worst you go back to the drawing board and figure out what went wrong, at best you are inspired to create again. In either instance, you learn to bridge the gap between your role as an account person and your role as a creative, and ultimately become better—way better—at both."

"I'd always heard that advertising was an industry of egos," Selbo wittily concludes. "For some of us, it has evolved into an industry of alter egos."

How to Present Like a Pro

In the Jumping Beyond Junior section, Brian Sheppard recommended presenting as much as possible and observing seniors do it in order to master "the pitch." Pointing out that some people in advertising are well into their career before learning this essential skill, Suzanne Pope offers advice for all levels in her Ihaveanidea.org article, "Giving Good Meeting."

"As you move from junior to intermediate and beyond, being able to sell great work becomes every bit as important as being able to do great work," Pope writes. Debunking the myth that being funny is a prerequisite to being a good presenter, she says it is more important to "clearly articulate how your ads will solve the client's business problem." The key is to prepare the presentation thoroughly "in accordance with the way clients actually think."

For Pope, "PowerPoint forced me to make my presentations more logical, more step-by-step, and thus, more client-friendly." She finds that PowerPoint satisfies clients' need for "logical checkpoints." Another advantage of this program is that often the ultimate decision maker at the client company does not attend a creative presentation, and PowerPoint ensures that client staff will present ideas to their boss in a logical way.

A low-tech aid that Pope suggests is backing up each campaign with a piece of paper stating the core idea concisely and objectively. As an example, she sums up the MasterCard "Priceless" campaign in a way that loses the emotion but directly explains the idea to clients: "Contrast everyday purchases with the things that money cannot buy to illustrate MasterCard's broad utility and empathy for its cardholders' priorities."

As for the problem of presenters' stage fright, Pope recommends props or visual aids that can draw the client's attention while giving the speaker a chance to focus his thoughts. But the most effective way to counter nervousness turns out to be the same as the way to get to Carnegie Hall: practice—in front of friends, colleagues, or alone in a room. Writing out the presentation word for word can help for the initial run-throughs, Pope says, but in front of clients the script should be memorized so the presenter can maintain eye contact with them.

For further coaching, Pope suggests skipping the expensive presentation courses and instead joining Toastmasters (http://www.toatmasters.org), an international organization of community-based groups that helps people be more comfortable with public speaking. And she offers some encouraging words: "We often think of clients as our adversaries, but it's just not true. When we go in there to present, our clients WANT us to succeed. They want to be sold."

What Is the Value of PR Accreditation?

Unlike job-hunting advertising professionals, such as creatives banking on their portfolios and those in other ad disciplines relying on their track records, public relations staffers can become accredited so potential employers will immediately recognize their level of achievement. In fact, there are two organizations that offer such accreditation for PR staffers who have been in the business at least five years: the Public Relations Society of America (PRSA) through its membership in the Universal Accreditation Board (UAB), and the International Business Communicators Association (IBCA).

The PRSA accreditation is called an APR (Accredited Public Relations) and is earned by passing an exam administered by the nine public relations organizations that make up the UAB. The comprehensive, computer-based exam tests competency in research, planning, implementing, and evaluating programs; ethics and law; communications models and theories; business literacy; management skills and issues; crisis communication management; media relations; and other knowledge. The UAB offers an online, interactive, multimedia course to help candidates prepare for the exam. The fee to take the exam is $385; several participating organizations in the UAB offer a discount to their members.

The IBCA offers an Accredited Business Communicator (ABC) designation to candidates who successfully complete a three-part evaluation: an application describing academic preparation and professional experiencing; a portfolio of two work samples that indicate the range of projects the candidate has been responsible for and his or her ability to strategize; and a four-and-a-half-hour examination with both oral and written sections.

The cost of the accreditation is $320 for IBCA members and $530 for nonmembers.

Not surprisingly, both the UAB and the IBCA tout the benefits of accreditation on their Web sites. "Based on the 2005 PR Week/Korn Ferry Salary Survey, accredited public relations professionals earn $102,031 versus $85,272 for those who are not accredited, or 20 percent more" is one of the quotes on the UAB home page. "IABC's biennial survey of the profession...shows that accredited members' average salary is significantly higher than that of non-accredited members," according to the IBCA's Web site. Besides the potential monetary gains, the organization's site states, "The ABC designation behind your name says that you have successfully met a global standard in organizational communication...Your work has been reviewed by your peers and has successfully stood the test that demonstrates you have a well-rounded problem-solving approach."

In her Examiner.com article "Considering Accreditation?" Valerie Simon quotes sources who also found obtaining the APR worthwhile. In Simon's article, Jessi Blakley, a senior account manager at the Florida-based consultancy Consensus Communications, is quoted as saying: "I am an ardent supporter of the accreditation process and would strongly encourage others to embrace the experience." Kirk Hazlett, APR, an assistant professor of communication at Curry College in Milton, Massachusetts, told Simon accreditation was useful because, "I needed a benchmark against which to measure future activities as I continued my upward climb in the profession."

However, in this same article Lindsay Olson, a partner and recruiter at Paradigm Staffing, a firm devoted exclusively to the PR and communications industry, says, "Solid experience and proven capabilities and accomplishments hold more weight than accreditation." According to Simon, Doug Serton, a senior associate at Heyman Associates, a New York City-based executive communications search firm, agrees: "Industry accreditation is not something that our clients specifically ask for in candidates."

In today's blogosphere, opinions on PR accreditation are divided. On her blog Communications Overtones (http://overtonecomm.blogspot.com), Kami Watson Huyse, APR, writes that the APR accreditation promotes public relations' ethical practice,

Keeping
in Touch

E-mail Etiquette: "The Ask"

Everyone in advertising, no matter how accomplished or what the job is, will have to ask for a colleague's help at some time. And in today's office, the request often comes via e-mail. In *Send: The Essential Guide to E-mail for Office and Home*, David Shipley and Will Schwalbe offer some tips for sending a request to an inbox politely and efficiently:

- The request should be reasonable.
- Use an attention-grabbing subject line and make the request early in the text.
- When writing at the suggestion of a mutual friend, mention that person's name up front.
- Focus: Ask for just one thing, or lots of things that are all related to a common end.
- Be brief, but specific enough to get all your questions answered in one reply.
- Create space around the text stating the request so it doesn't get lost.
- "When making a large request of someone's time, it can be helpful to propose a smaller request first."
- Those in a position of power should be careful not to ask for something without realizing it. A boss may write a musing like "Wouldn't it be nice to know..." and unintentionally set off a flurry of activity in her department.
- Be up-front: Don't hide your request in a note that's seemingly just a friendly letter.
- Send the e-mail at a convenient time for your recipient, like regular business hours. Sending it an odd hour in an attempt to get the person's attention can wind up being annoying.
- Be polite. "Because of e-mail's inherent lack of affect, a little flattery never hurts, and it's sometimes necessary to be extravagantly polite."
- If you haven't received a response to your e-mail, you can resend your original note. But acknowledge it's a second attempt, and apologize.

management function, and a link to organizational goals. Writing on his blog PR-Squared (http://www.pr-squared.com) in response to Watson Huyse's pro-accreditation post, Todd Defren says, "Accreditation only legitimizes one organization's (the PRSA) view of what is entailed by 'Public Relations.' In this dawning era of new media, the PR person's role is (thankfully!) more fluid and unknown than ever. This fluidity is an opportunity" that would be lost "by force-fitting PR pros into the required learning and roles defined by a standards body." Defren finds the most convincing proof that accreditation isn't necessary right in his own PR agency of over 75 people. "None have 'APR' affixed to their business cards, yet there's not a single one whom I wouldn't trust to give solid PR counsel to a client."

In "Here's what's rising from the grave of traditional PR," a post on her Brazen Careerist blog (http://blog.penelopetrunk.com), Penelope Trunk quotes Defren on social media's effect on PR and describes a changing industry in which the current accreditations may be outdated. Where once the PR specialist pitched a story to contacts in traditional media, Trunk sets out the new playing field: "Here's how it works: The online influencers are on Twitter. They send traffic to blogs and Facebook and StumbleUpon. And those people e-mail their friends, in community-wide missives, and that's how something becomes viral."

But even better than a viral campaign are "real conversations" among consumers online, Trunk says. So instead of using PR agencies "to work their magic on outdated media gatekeepers" Trunk suggests that companies "train passionate employees and customers to have authentic conversations about the brand." If the use of social media continues to grow in the future as many predict, the question facing PR professionals may not be whether or not to be accredited, but what their role will be in these consumer conversations.

A Truly Creative Job Search

Advertising creatives spend their days thinking of new ways to make their client's products stand out in the marketplace. So why shouldn't they use their skills to make themselves more memorable among employers when job hunting?

In "Job Hunting Guerilla-Style," an article posted on Ihaveanidea. org, Brendan Watson describes the results of that line of reasoning when he and his creative partner set out to find work in advertising.

Watson makes it clear that none of their "guerilla" tactics should be considered as a substitute for "the combination of hard work, thick skin, persistence, timing and being a generally good person with a great book." But then a lot of job hunters in advertising meet these criteria; this creative team's unexpected, personal touches helped them stand out.

While Watson and his partner, Jana, were at the Silverhammer agency under a contract that was about to run out, they heard Ian Mirlin, chief creative officer at Young & Rubican, speak at an agency event. Mirlin referred to the *Peanuts* character Charlie Brown, pointing out how he always played baseball with his glove down, never ready to catch the ball.

Determined to make an impression on Mirlin, the next day Watson and Jana left a box on his desk. "Inside was a baseball glove, with our names etched into it and a small card with a picture of Charlie Brown that read 'Ready and Waiting,'" Watson writes.

When the team was meeting with the agency Taxi's associate creative director, Lance Martin, he said he liked their work but was not sure if they "had space for them"— meaning physical space, since the agency had beefed up for special projects, "Well, if space is the only problem, then we'll work on the street," Watson and Jana said. "Lance laughed it off," not suspecting that two days later the guerilla creatives be would be sitting in a makeshift office on the sidewalk outside his window, Watson recounts. "There we sat in the rain...with desks, chairs, books, decorations, a computer and a printer. We had an 'inter-office' memo delivered to Lance which read, 'If space is your problem, then we've solved it. Please look out your window.'" Martin and some colleagues braved the bad weather to ask Watson and Jana in for "a coffee and a creative brief." They spent the next few days lending a hand on a project for a brand new client.

Sending a "cookie-gram" from a professional service could be a nice way to thank an agency for a meeting and wish them luck on a new account. But Watson and Jana wanted to do something more personal for the creative director at Bensimon Byrne in Toronto, who was bidding on the Hyundai account. So they baked their own cookie in the shape of Hyundai's "flying H" logo and packaged it in a "Brendan & Jana" branded box. First they received a thank-you call, and then three weeks later got another call with a job offer they accepted.

INTERVIEW

The Strategic Career-Self

Penelope Trunk
National columnist and author, *Brazen Careerist*

What would you say to someone who has been working at a first job in advertising or PR for a few years and now wants to advance?

My advice would be the same as for young professionals in most any field. You have to learn how make your boss's life easier. How do you do this? First you have to figure out what you're really good at. Then you can use that strength to fill in where your boss or the rest of the team is lacking. You might be a good idea person and networker, which are good skills to have in PR, or maybe you're not.

When you're starting a career you may first find a number of things that you suck at. But search for a strength, and when you find it, own it.

It's been said that people in Generation Y may have three to five careers in a lifetime. Instead of just trying to get a better position, they should be looking for a job they're really interested in and that will stretch them.

In your columns you have talked about the value of job hopping and having breaks in your résumé to plan career moves. Won't some more traditional managers have a problem with this?

Then don't work for a boss who has a problem with job-hopping. Part of being successful is figuring out who you want to work for.

Are there times when it still makes sense to work your way up the ladder in one company?

Yes, if you're a very low-risk person. But the real road to HELL, and I'd spell that in all caps, is a career path that never gets you out of middle management. You might have to make a number of lateral moves to get the skills and experience you need to escape that dead end.

You have written that "Mentoring is the new currency." What do you mean by that?

Just that getting the usual raise of a few percent is B.S. You should say, Instead of the money I want these three mentors in the company who I think can help me learn. Or, Give me a certain type of training, or a challenging project.

As far as picking a mentor, young working people are great at asking people for help. They can select one or two mentors and see how they work out. When you find you really click with someone, you can then limit yourself to working with him or her.

I have read your advice about taking the initiative to learn all you can about the field you are working in and even doing side projects in another field while you are employed full time, so you will be more versatile. Do you think Generation Y is up for making all that extra effort?
Generation Y is the most productive group of workers. Some of these kids are just out of my league! Besides, just working a full-time job is not that hard. It's much harder to answer career questions like, Who are you? How much money do you really need to live on?

I see the value of answering the question, "What do you do?" with a story, as you have recommended for networking. But do entry-level people really have enough experience to construct a story of their own?
It's probably harder for older people who have had as many as 10 jobs but never found anything they really enjoyed doing. Knowing your story is about finding your strength, as we talked about earlier. And your story changes as you grow and new things you're doing become more important to you.

I know you are very much in favor of blogging and that your blog is one of the most helpful for career and life planning. Do you think writing a blog is more important for certain positions in advertising, like creatives, than others?
No, everybody should blog! You can express your ideas about your career, whatever it is. You'll learn from the responses you get and will improve by taking criticisms to heart. Also, because of the way Google is designed blogs always come up first when people do a search for your name. So if you maintain a polished and informative blog, people looking for you online will get a very good first impression.

"Focus on the company, not the job," you have suggested. Please expand on that.
Your strengths and weaknesses are independent of any particular company. You want to go with the company that will give the most training for your long-term career.

The More Mentors the Merrier

Professionals who have mentors are twice as likely to be promoted as those who do not, according to Ellen Fagenson Eland, professor at George Mason University. Gerard Roche, senior chairman at the recruiting firm Heidrick & Struggles, adds that "Executives who have had mentors have earned more money at a younger age," and "are happier with their career progress and derive greater pleasure from their work."

These are just two of the sources cited by Penelope Trunk on her career-advice blog to support her strong belief in the importance of mentors to younger workers in any field. In fact, on her blog, Penelope Trunk's Brazen Careerist (http://blog.penelopetrunk.com), Trunk has had more than 20 posts on the subject of mentoring.

Here is a summary of a particularly helpful one, "Seven steps to finding and keeping a mentor":

Pick a potential mentor. Besides choosing someone you admire and can talk to, consider Trunk's opinion that "...the most effective mentor is someone approximately five years ahead of you in your career." Why? Someone in this position "will know how to navigate your organization at the spot you're in, and...remember what it is like to be where you are."

Prepare good questions. "What makes a good question? It should reveal that you are both directed and driven." Trunk also recommends specific questions that show "you understand the mentor's expertise and you can use it well."

"Don't expect miracles." Instead of expecting a mentor to "rescue your whole career," try to appear like the type of on-track "rising star" who people want to mentor. "Ask, 'What skills should I develop to earn an education policy analyst job with a Senator?' rather than, 'Can you get me a job with a Senator?'"

"Be a good listener." Ask a question, then listen. "If the mentor needs to know more, he'll ask." Trunk cautions that talking too much might "scare your mentor away."

"Prove you're serious." Demonstrate this "by implementing the advice your mentor gave, showing the result, and then going back for more." If your mentor suggests getting on a certain project, "get yourself there, do a good job, and report back to your mentor that you are grateful for the advice because you were able to learn a lot and shine."

One mentor is not enough. "Each person needs a few mentors, because no mentor lasts forever, and each has a different expertise."

Trunk gives the example of two of her best mentors: One who helped her "fit in with the guys" at a company where she was the only woman in management, and another who helped her balance work and children.

"Give back." Becoming a mentor yourself will help you find out what makes a protégée difficult, so you can avoid doing those things with your mentor. "You'll also discover why helping someone else grow is so rewarding, which will give you the courage to ask people to help you."

A Media Manager's Hiring Criteria

Since Barry Lowenthal first got into the media-planning side of the ad business more than 18 years ago, so much has changed that even his discipline has a new name: channel planning. In "What I Look For in a Candidate," an article on Talentzoo.com, Lowenthal lays out the skills and knowledge needed to break into changing media departments today.

Lowenthal recalls how he was coached to answer the question of why he wanted a job in media with the line, "I wanted a career that allowed me to express my creative side and leverage my affinity for numbers." Now sitting on the other side of the desk as president of the Media Kitchen, he says, "We still look for evidence that the person can add up a column of numbers, but we are just as eager to learn about his or her pop culture obsessions." His channel planners get technical support for managing data; it is becoming more important for them to spot trends through a study of publications and Web sites.

Having long been a believer that candidates who worked their way through college would have the kind of work ethic his agency needs, Lowenthal now thinks curiosity is just as important: "I believe people who are extremely curious about the world they live in understand how people communicate and the role brands play in facilitating communication."

Media departments still perform the day-to-day tasks of analyzing competitive spending, posting media buys, and issuing insertion orders. But they can be even more valuable to clients by using new technology and more channels "to deploy the right message to the right place at the right time." Lowenthal says that means planners should be as familiar with celebrity blogs and planograms (diagrams of where merchandise should be displayed in retail) as they are with a calculator. In other words, "The people who succeed in today's media agencies need to be media anthropologists as much as media planners."

You Have Arrived! Now Keep Staff from Leaving

Most of this chapter is about planning to do well and get ahead in advertising. But once you accomplish that and find yourself managing creatives, part of your job is getting the really talented ones to plan on staying with you.

Not surprisingly, "keeping salaries competitive is a good start," according to Mandy Gilbert, director of Creative Niche Inc., in her Ihaveanidea.org article on retaining creative talent. But there are other, less tangible but important factors that staff often consider:

"Be willing to bend." Flexibility with the perks, benefits, and incentives you offer can help build loyalty. It is important to tailor these accommodations to each person's situation, while still remaining fair to the whole group.

"Keep an ear to the ground." Be aware of your staff members' concerns and problems by talking with them individually and holding frequent, open staff meetings. Lay the groundwork by creating an atmosphere of trust and responsiveness.

Offer a career path within the company. Find out your staff members' career goals and try to help them meet these without leaving the company. However, the organization then has to be open to options like letting people advance without having to manage people.

Challenge staff to stretch. Creative staff do not like to do the "same old same old." So offer them "new and interesting projects that can broaden their expertise, and encourage your staff members to experiment with cutting-edge techniques."

Help your talent grow. Subsidize continuing education courses and encourage staff to attend trade shows and industry events.

"Invest in equipment." Creatives want to be up-to-date with the latest computer models and software. So provide this "strong retention incentive."

Do PR for the agency. Continuously make the case for why it is a great place to work and grow.

"Avoid superstar fizzle." It is tempting to keep assigning projects to the best staff, but that can lead to burnout. "Instead, save the most interesting, high-profile projects for your top talent." During peak times you can hire freelancers rather than overburden your key staff.

Do more with décor. Creative people are naturally more aware of office aesthetics. So the standard "identical cubes with fluorescent lighting" may be a turnoff. Try to introduce more inspiring décor and encourage staff to do the same.

Praise is free. Whenever staff members do a good job, be sure to acknowledge them.

Leaders Must Keep Learning

What do Bill Bradley, Kurt Vonnegut, and Steve Jobs have to do with advertising? They all have something to teach ad managers, according to "Leadership: The Continuous Improvement," an article by Greg Taucher and Stacey Prenner posted on TalentZoo.com (http://www.talentzoo.com).

Taucher and Prenner begin their piece with a reference to another famous person, Peter F. Drucker, who in 1999 wrote that to succeed in "the emerging knowledge economy" people must "know their strengths, their values and under what circumstances they best perform." Now that the knowledge economy has emerged, followed by the online-business model, Taucher and Prenner propose that another term should be added to Drucker's qualifications: "collaboration," or "being able to effectively influence, without all the trappings of politics and the blinding use of 'I,' a number of individuals who may not necessarily report to you...work in the same marketing services discipline as you...or even the same company as you."

The authors write that in this new economy the ability to lead is not dependent on age and experience as much as "one's own practice in the pursuit of continuous improvement." However, a would-be leader must first find his area of expertise. Or, as former New York Knicks star and former U.S. Senator Bill Bradley once answered a question about using your innate talent, "You always have to know where you are."

While Taucher and Prenner encourage developing managers to learn as much as they can about rapidly changing marketing services, they challenge them to take the additional step of putting their ideas into action. That's where Kurt Vonnegut comes in: He is quoted as saying, "New knowledge is the most valuable commodity on earth so long as you do something with it."

The key to implementing an idea is to include "the commercial side of the equation," or restated, to back it up with a "solid business case." Leaders must also make sure they have the support of the "ops guys" (legal, finance, sales, procurement, logistics, retail, HR). For a good model of how to get these groups behind an idea, Taucher and Prenner suggest watching Steve Jobs present a new Apple product on YouTube.

Summing up with a key distinction, the authors point out "it will be your leadership style (not your management style) that will inspire those around you to develop stronger results-oriented partnerships."

Staying in the Game: Against Ageism in Advertising

In *Pick Me*, Nancy Vonk and Janet Kestin, sum up the situation with a clever chapter heading: "Age(ism): Is 39 the New 65?" While most people's careers, they write, are 40 years long, "Most advertising people's working lives are roughly half that." The short-lived career is especially true for creatives, who are apt to burn out due to the pressures of "creative on demand."

To counter this trend, Steffan Postaer wrote "The Creative Athlete: Winning at Any Age," for TalentZoo.com (http://www.talent-zoo.com). In a sense, the article is an extended pep talk for creatives, urging them to stay in the game by staying at the top of their game.

Postaer runs through the list of sports metaphors that have long been part of the ad business. Good ideas are "plays that work." Competing for business is called a "pitch." "Each agency fields a 'team.'" Euro RSCG, Postaer's agency, was an "underdog" when it opened in Chicago, but eventually won in the "minor leagues" with small accounts and then in "the bigs."

Agencies want to be on the same roster as their clients. "As creative partners we can help them field a better team," Postaer believes. "When we kick off a new campaign the game begins. By the 4th quarter we better have results."

The concept of being a "creative athlete" is another way of stating the axiom "Use it or lose it." "Working out our creative muscles is key to staying healthy. A writer writes. Books, scripts, poems, blogs. Not just copy," Postaer says. "Art directors pick up a paintbrush or camera. And you'd better know your way around Photoshop."

Postaer encourages his peers to stay in shape, both mentally and physically, not just to keep playing but to excel at the ad game. His egalitarian perspective is "a youthful approach to our business that diffuses political correctness, allowing talent to shine no matter its color or sex."

What Veterans Wish They Had Known as Rookies

Jim Lauerman, a 30-year veteran of the advertising business, begins his article on advice to younger professionals in a humble and enlightening way. "Once you feel you have it figured out...that you now are the teacher, get out" of the business, he writes in "The Top 10 Things You Need to Know If You Want to Spend Some Serious Time in Advertising," TalentZoo.com (http://www.talentzoo.com). Neither Lauerman nor any of the other accomplished ad men and women quoted here would claim to be experts on careers. But with their accumulated experience of a couple hundred years, they offer a good idea of what to expect, what to avoid, and what else besides luck can help you succeed.

What Lauerman says "you need to know" can be summarized as follows:

- There are two kinds of people in the advertising-agency business: "those who love advertising and those who love the business of advertising." Since agencies need both to be successful, Lauerman writes the two groups have to collaborate and each one must learn to appreciate the "other side."
- Good communication skills are key. This means more than writing well and is beyond being "slick." "Being able to communicate meaningfully, eye-to-eye across the desk, in terms that mean something to your client and your team members, is critical."
- "Beware of becoming a dinosaur." Since the ad industry "thrives on energy, invention, and change," you have to make the effort to stay current in technology and other developments."
- Be a problem solver who improves a client's business "and people will think you're brilliant."
- Be a "coach and confidence builder rather than a judge and critic."
- "You can't die on every hill." Pick your battles instead of arguing over every element in an ad.
- Advertising is "a business of making good first impressions"—on clients and on their customers.
- "You'll end up knowing more about more businesses than you ever thought you would."
- The more life experience you have had before getting into advertising, the better you will be at contributing to your clients' successes.

All the agency disciplines require "truckloads of creativity." But because of all the requirements of each one, "You'll spend less time 'creating' than you think you will." In their book *Pick Me*, Nancy Vonk and Janet Kestin have a chapter titled, "What I Know Now That I Wish I Knew Then." Some of the pithier responses that creative gurus gave to this query were:

- Bob Barrie: "It never gets easy." "Don't make career decisions based on monetary gain." (Others agreed there are more important considerations, like "love what you do.")
- Kestin: "The well won't run dry." "Know what you believe." (Or, get your ethics straight.) "Don't let the business become your world."
- Lorraine Tao: "You don't have to be an extrovert to be successful in advertising."
- Vonk: "Be a true partner to your clients." "Long hours don't always translate to quality thinking." To art directors regarding shooting TV commercials: "Don't hand over the reins to directors despite all pressure to do so."
- Rick Boyko: "It's always easier to beg forgiveness than to ask for permission." In other words: If you have a good idea, what are you waiting for?

Chapter 5

Talk Like a Pro

AAAA American Association of Advertising Agencies.

above the line (ATL) Any advertising technique that focuses on general media such as TV, cinema, radio, print, and Internet. See "Below the line."

accumulation An audience-counting method in which each person exposed to a specific ad is counted once within a certain time period.

ad copy The text in print ads or spoken script in broadcast media.

adjacencies Time periods immediately before and after a television program, normally used as a commercial break.

adnorm A measure of readership averages for print publications over a two-year period, used as a baseline for comparing specific ads.

advergaming Packaging a message within a computer game to advertise a product or organization.

advertising allowance Money provided by a manufacturer to a distributor for the purpose of advertising a specific product or brand.

advertising budget The amount of money a company or other organization has to spend on advertising.

advertising elasticity The relationship between a change in advertising budget and the resulting change in product sales.

advertising-page exposure A measure of the opportunity for readers to see a particular print advertisement, whether or not they actually look at the ad.

advertising plan   An explicit outline of advertising campaign's goals, how to accomplish them, and how to determine whether or not the campaign met them.

advertising research   Research conducted to improve the effectiveness of advertising. It may focus on a specific ad or campaign, or on gaining a more general understanding of how advertising works or how consumers use the information in advertising

advertorial   An advertisement in a print publication that has the appearance of a news article or editorial.

advocacy advertising   Promoting a position on a political, controversial or other social issue.

affirmative disclosure   A disclosure of information in an advertisement, required by the Federal Trade Commission or other authority, that frequently admits to some limitation in the product or the offer being made.

agency commission   The agency's fee for designing and placing advertisements. Historically calculated as 15 percent of the amount spent to place the ad in various media, in recent years the commission has in many cases become negotiable.

AIDA   Stands for Attention, Interest, Desire, and Action. This is a historical model of the progression of advertising's effects on consumers.

aided recall   A research method frequently used to determine what consumers remember about an advertisement.

a la carte services   Agency services that a client purchases individually as needed.

ANA   Association of National Advertisers. An association whose members are companies that advertise their products or services.

answer print   The final edited version of a television commercial, presented to the client for approval.

Arbitron   Television and radio rating service that publishes regular reports on ads for selected markets.

area of dominant influence (ADI)   A geographic designation used by Arbitron to specify which counties are in a specific television market.

art proof   The artwork for an ad that is submitted for client approval.

audience   The number of people or households exposed to an ad, whether or not they actually saw or heard it.

audience duplication   The number of people who saw or heard more than one of the programs or publications in which an ad was placed. Advertisers trying to reach as many different consumers as possible want this measure to be low, while those who think they will sell the most by focusing on a sample group seek a high audience-duplication rate.

Audilog   Used by A.C. Nielsen as a means of rating television shows, this is a diary kept by selected audience members to record which television programs they watched.

Audimeter   An electronic recording device used by A.C. Nielsen to track when a television set is in use, and to what station it is set.

Audit Bureau of Circulations (ABC)   A company that audits the circulation of print publications to insure that reported circulation figures are accurate.

availability   Amount of time on radio or television that is available to be purchased for ads set to air at a specific time.

average audience (AA)   The number of homes or people tuned to a television program during an average minute, or the number of people who viewed an average issue of a print publication.

bait advertising   Advertising a product at a very low price, while knowing it is almost impossible to obtain the product for that price. See *cease-and-desist order.*

bandwidth   The amount of data (text, video, sound, images, animations) that can be moved through an Internet connection. Typically measured in bits per second (bps).

barter   Exchanging merchandise, or something other than money, for advertising time or space.

billboard   (1) An outdoor sign or poster; (2) Sponsor identification at the beginning or end of a television show.

bleed   To allow a picture or ad to extend beyond margins to the edges of a printed page.

blow-in card   An advertisement, subscription request, or other printed card "blown" into a publication rather than bound into it.

blueline   A blue line drawn on a print-ready layout to indicate where a page will be cut.

body copy   The main text of a print ad, as opposed to the headline.

boutique   A relatively small agency that provides a limited service, such as creative work, rather than the full range of services clients need.

Fast Facts

From Jargon to Jokes

Commenting on the advertising industry's internal lingo, Dan Goldgeier, an ad copywriter and columnist for TalentZoo.com (http://www.talentzoo.com), says, "...I find the language we use internally to be very bizarre." Goldgeier makes his point in two columns posted several years apart: "On Killer Books and Hard-Hitting Execution" and "The Importance of Filtering Actionable Jargon Into Buckets." As these edited versions of Goldgeier's definitions show, his satirical view of advertising jargon takes it from "bizarre" to funny:

Brief—"Never seen one that was."

Buckets—"Sometimes, during a brainstorm, the downpour of ideas becomes such a vast pool of genius that someone needs to mop it all up and place it into a number of 'buckets.' Hopefully without spilling any of that brilliance."

Change agent—"Change doesn't need an agent. Or an advocate. Most people don't like change. But things just change, whether you like it or not. Go with it."

Direct marketing—"This is a cute euphemism for 'junk mail' or 'spam.' ...Your e-mails and junk mail may have my name directly inserted into them, but they're still mostly auto-generated, and I throw them directly into the trash."

Deliverable—"Actually, this is a bad one. A really bad one. Agencies aren't paid for their thinking, or to propose ideas that might improve a client's business, like beefing up customer service or retraining employees. No, ad agencies get paid for deliverables, like a pizza parlor. Would you like a direct mail piece with everything in it and extra logos to go? Because you can bill a client for that deliverable."

brand development index (BDI) A comparison of the percent of a brand's sales in a market to the percent of the national population in that same market.

branded content The integration of brands into the content of various media, as well as the creation of original content centered on brands.

Edgy–"Somebody...already addressed this term pretty effectively. He said that when something has an edge, someone is bound to get cut. The moral here is that if you go to present an 'edgy' idea to a client, bring some tourniquets. Remember: Edgy ideas are not always killer ideas. And if you fall on your sword for an edgy idea, you might be the one who gets killed. Or fired."

Killer–"Describing any great ad as 'killer' always perplexed me. If an ad is a killer, well, does it mean the ad's 'target' would be rendered dead by watching or reading the ad? Are we talking about advertising or quail hunting? Killer diseases are bad....Why are killer ads good?"

Loyalty program–"Sorry, there's no such thing. I save 30 cents off a gallon of milk at Kroger because I have a plastic card on my key-chain that says I'm a member of a 'loyalty program.' Nice discount, but it doesn't make me loyal. Any store that's cheaper, closer, or better will get my loyalty, at least for the day."

Shop–"Ad agencies are commonly referred to as 'shops.' This term has an old-world feel, as if ad people were artisans like cobblers or black-smiths, crafting great ads in our 'shop.' But in my experience, clients tend to dictate what they want, and get it exactly how they want it..."

Thought leader–"Back in high school, if you told people you were cool, you weren't. Same goes for calling yourself a 'thought leader.' If you have to go around telling people you are one, you aren't."

Viral–"I don't know who first looked at their marketing budget and said, 'Now, if only we could be as successful as AIDS or herpes. Let's do something the great unwashed consumers could spread without more media dollars.' And alas, viral marketing caught on. No actual viral campaign has spread quite like the mere concept of doing a viral marketing campaign has...I'm developing an immunity to viral marketing. I suspect most consumers are, too."

brand manager   Person who has marketing responsibilities for a specific brand.

brand name   Name used to distinguish a product, an entire product line, or even a company from its competitors.

broadside   A promotion that is printed on a single large sheet of paper, usually on only one side of the paper.

buried position   Hard-to-find spots among other ads in a print publication.

business-to-business (B to B or B2B) advertising   Advertising directed to other businesses as opposed to consumers.

caption   The text accompanying an illustration or photograph.

car card   A poster placed in buses, subways, etc. Also called a bus card.

card rate   Cost of advertising on a broadcast station or in a print publication as listed on a "rate card."

category development index (CDI)   A comparison of the percent of sales of a product category in a market, to the percent of population in that market.

cease-and-desist order   An order by the Federal Trade Commission requiring an advertiser to stop running a deceptive or unfair advertisement, campaign, or claim, such as bait advertising.

channels of distribution   The routes used by a company to distribute its products, such as wholesalers, retailers, and mail order.

circulation (circ)   For a print publication, the average number of copies distributed. For outdoor advertising, the total number of people who have an opportunity to observe a billboard or poster.

classified advertising   Print advertising that is limited to certain classes of goods and services, and usually limited in size and content.

clearance   Review of an advertisement for legal, ethical, and taste standards before accepting the ad for publication.

closing date   The day final copy and other materials must be submitted in order to appear in a specific issue or time slot.

coincidental survey   A survey of viewers or listeners conducted during a broadcast program.

collateral materials   Print matter like sales brochures, catalogs, and spec sheets, generally delivered to consumers (or dealers) by a sales person in support of a selling message.

color proof   A preliminary full-color print of a finished advertisement, used to evaluate its final appearance.

color separation   A full-color ad normally is generated through printing of four separate colors: yellow, cyan, magenta, and black. The color separation consists of four separate screens, one for each of those colors.

column inch   A unit of measure newspapers use to sell ad space consisting of the width in columns, and the depth in inches. For example, an ad that is three standard columns wide and five inches deep would be 15 column inches.

combination rate   A special pricing arrangement for purchasing space or time in more than one media in a package deal. This is frequently offered where different vehicles share a common owner.

commercial advertising   Advertising that involves commercial interests rather than advocating a social or political cause.

comparative advertising   An ad that explicitly compares one product brand to a competitive brand.

competitive parity   A method of determining an advertising budget that is designed to maintain the current "share of voice."

comprehensive layout (comp)   A rough layout of an ad designed for presentation only but done in enough detail to indicate what the finished ad will look.

consent order (consent decree)   A Federal Trade Commission order by which an advertiser agrees to make changes in an advertisement or campaign without having a legal hearing.

consumer advertising   Advertising directed at people who will use the product themselves, rather than at a business or dealer.

consumer behavior   How people behave when obtaining, using, and disposing of (or ceasing to use) products and services.

consumerism   (1) Advocating the rights of consumers, as against the efforts of advertisers. (2) The emphasis of advertising and marketing efforts on creating consumers. (These two definitions are almost opposite in meaning, but the former is commonly used today, while the latter was common prior to the 1970s.)

consumer jury test   A method of testing advertisements that involves asking consumers to compare, rank, and otherwise evaluate the ads.

continuous advertising   Scheduling advertisements to appear regularly, even during times when consumers are not likely to purchase the product or service, so that they are constantly reminded of the brand.

controlled (qualified) circulation   Publications, generally business-oriented, that are delivered (usually free) only to readers who have some special qualifications. Generally, publications are free to the qualified recipients.

cooperative (co-op) program (cooperative advertising) A system by which ad costs are divided between two or more parties. Usually offered by manufacturers to their wholesalers or retailers to prompt them to advertise the product.

copy All written text or spoken words in an advertisement.

copy testing Research to determine consumer responses to the ad.

cost per thousand (CPM) The cost, per 1,000 people reached, of buying advertising space in a given medium.

Council of Better Business Bureaus (CBBB) A national organization of local business bureaus.

creative strategy An outline of the ad message that should be conveyed, to whom, and with what tone. This provides the guiding principles for copywriters and art directors who are assigned to develop the advertisement.

creatives The art directors and copywriters in an ad agency.

cumes Used by A.C. Nielsen as an abbreviation for net cumulative audience. Refers to the number of unduplicated people or homes in a broadcast program's audience within a specified time period.

cutting A film editing technique that creates a quick transition from one scene to another.

DAGMAR A process of establishing goals for an ad campaign so that it is possible to determine whether or not the goals have been met. It stands for Defining Advertising Goals for Measured Advertising Results.

dailies Also called "rushes," these are called dailies because the film typically is viewed from a single day's shooting, even if the final commercial or program will take many days or weeks of shooting.

daypart Broadcast media divide the day into several standard time periods, each of which is called a "daypart." Cost of purchasing advertising time on a vehicle varies by the daypart selected.

decay constant An estimate of the decline in product sales if advertising were discontinued.

deceptive advertising FTC definition: A representation, omission, act, or practice that is likely to mislead consumers acting reasonably under the circumstances. To be regulated, however, a deceptive claim must also be material. See *materiality.*

demographics Basic objective descriptive classifications of consumers, such as their age, sex, income, education, size of household, and ownership of home. This does not include classification by subjective attitudes or opinions of consumers. See *psychographics*.

direct mail   Marketing communications delivered directly to a prospective purchaser via the U.S. Postal Service or a private delivery company.

direct marketing   Sending a promotional message directly to consumers, rather than via a mass medium. Includes methods such as direct mail and telemarketing.

direct response   Promotions that permit or request consumers to respond directly to the advertiser, by mail, telephone, e-mail, or some other means of communication. Some practitioners use this as a synonym for direct marketing.

distributor   A company or person that distributes a manufacturer's goods to retailers. The terms "wholesaler" and "jobber" are sometimes used to describe distributors.

drive time   Used in radio, this refers to morning and afternoon times when consumers are driving to and from work. See *daypart.*

dummy   A copy (xerographic duplicate) of an ad, or even blank sheets of paper, provided to a printer or artist as an example of the size, color, or other aspect of the ad to be produced.

earned rate   A discounted media rate, based on volume or frequency of media placement.

eighty-twenty rule   A rule-of-thumb that for the typical product category, 80 percent of the products sold will be consumed by 20 percent of the customers.

end user   The person who actually uses a product, whether or not he or she is the one who purchased the product.

eye tracking   A research method that determines what part of an advertisement consumers look at by tracking the pattern of their eye movements.

family brand   A brand name that is used for more than one product, known as a family of products.

FCC   Federal Communications Commission. The federal agency responsible for regulating broadcast and electronic communications.

fixed-sum-per-unit method   A method of determining an advertising budget based directly on the number of units sold.

flighting   A media schedule that involves more advertising at certain times and less advertising during others.

focus group interview A research method that brings together a small group of consumers to discuss the product or advertising, under the guidance of a trained interviewer.

font A typeface style, such as Helvetica or Times Roman, in a single size. A single font includes all 26 letters, along with punctuation, numbers, and other characters.

four-color process A printing process that combines differing amounts of each of four colors (red, yellow, blue and black) to provide a full-color print.

four Ps Stands for product, price, place (i.e., distribution), and promotion. This is also known as the **marketing mix**.

franchised position An ad position in a periodic publication, like the back cover, that an advertiser claims for permanent or long-term right of use.

free-standing insert (FSI) An advertisement or group of ads inserted—but not bound—in a print publication, on pages that contain only the ads and are separate from any editorial or entertainment matter.

frequency Number of times an average person or home is exposed to a media vehicle (or group of vehicles), within a given time period.

FTC Federal Trade Commission. The federal agency primarily responsible for regulating national advertising.

full position An ad that is surrounded by reading matter in a newspaper, making it more likely consumers will read it. This is a highly desirable location for an ad.

full-service agency An agency that handles all aspects of the advertising process, including planning, design, production, and placement. Today, full-service generally suggests that the agency also handles other aspects of marketing communication, such as public relations, sales promotion, and direct marketing.

galley proof A typeset copy of an ad or editorial material, before it is made into pages for final production.

galvanometer test A research method that measures physiological changes in consumers when asked a question or shown some stimulus material like an ad.

gatefold Double or triple-size pages, generally in magazines, that fold out into a large advertisement.

grid card A broadcast media rate card that lists rates on a grid, according to the time periods that might be selected for the ad.

On the Cutting
Edge

Experiential Marketing

"Cold, provided by winter. Warmth, provided by Stove Top." That was the headline on posters placed inside 10 bus shelters in Chicago during December 2008. Commuters coming in from the cold could thank Kraft Foods, makers of Stove Top stuffing, for providing the welcome heat in these shelters. But as Stewart Elliott points out in his article "Hot Food, and Air, at Bus Stops," in the *New York Times*, Kraft was not just looking for gratitude; the company was hoping for increased Stove Top sales by employing a new ad technique known as experiential marketing.

The heated shelters were intended to have consumers experience the warm feeling they associate with stuffing, according to Kraft. The Stove Top campaign is an example of how this increasingly popular marketing tool tries "to entice consumers to experience products or brands tangibly rather than bombard them with pitches," Elliott writes.

To enhance the multi-sensory experience, Kraft gave samples of a new variety of Stove Top to commuters at half of the heated shelters. The samples supported another campaign goal of getting people to think of Stove Top as an everyday meal, according to a Kraft marketing executive.

Other examples of experiential marketing in the fourth quarter of 2008 were Procter & Gamble's annual sponsorship of restrooms in Times Square, on behalf of brands like Charmin toilet paper, and temporary pop-up stores with samples marketing Meow Mix cat food, Unilever's Suave hair care line, and the United States Potato Board.

As with other new types of advertising, marketers must be sure experiential ads get attention but do not annoy consumers. Elliott cites an earlier campaign in which the California Milk Processor Board placed scent strips that smelled like chocolate chip cookies in bus shelters in San Francisco. The strips were meant to stimulate the desire for a glass of milk to go with the cookies. But the campaign was abruptly ended when critics said the scent was inappropriate in public places and could set off allergic reactions.

gross impressions Total number of unduplicated people or households represented by a given media schedule.

gross rating points (GRPs) **Reach** times average frequency. This is a measure of the advertising weight delivered by a **vehicle** or vehicles within a given time period.

guaranteed circulation A media rate that comes with a guarantee that the publication will achieve a certain circulation.

halftone A black-and-white photograph or illustration reproduced by representing various shades of gray as a series of black and white dots.

hologram A three-dimensional photograph or illustration created with an optical process that uses lasers.

horizontal publications Business publications designed to appeal to people of similar interests or responsibilities in a variety of companies or industries.

house agency An advertising agency owned and operated by an advertiser, which handles its own account.

households using television (HUT) The number of households in a given market watching television at a certain time.

house organ A publication owned and operated by an advertiser and used to promote its products or services.

image advertising Promoting the image or general perception of a product or service, rather than its functional attributes. Commonly used for differentiating brands of parity products.

industrial advertising A form of business-to-business advertising (see above), it is aimed at manufacturers and typically promotes parts, equipment, and raw materials used in the manufacturing process.

infomercial A commercial that is very similar in appearance to a news program, talk show, or other non-advertising program. The broadcast equivalent of an **advertorial**.

insert An advertisement, collection of advertisements, or other promotional matter published by an advertiser or group of advertisers and inserted in a magazine or newspaper.

insertion Refers to an ad in a print publication.

insertion order An agency's or advertiser's authorization for a publisher to run a specific ad in a specific print publication on a certain date at a specified price.

institutional advertising Advertising to promote an institution or organization, rather than a product or service, in order to create public support and goodwill.

integrated Marketing Communication (IMC)   A
management concept designed to make all aspects of marketing
communication (advertising, sales promotion, public relations,
and direct marketing) work together as a unified campaign.

international advertising   Advertising a product or service in a
country other than where it originates.

island position   Placement of a print ad that is completely
surrounded by editorial material, or a broadcast ad surrounded
by program content, with no adjoining advertisements to
compete for audience attention.

jingle   A short song, usually mentioning a brand or product
benefit, used in a commercial.

keeper   A premium used to induce a consumer to take some
action, such as completing a survey or trying a product.

kerning   Spacing between the letters of a word.

layout   A drawing that indicates the relative positions of the
elements (headline, photo, logo, body copy) of an ad.

leave-behind   A premium left with prospective customers by a
sales person to remind them of the product or service being sold.

lifestyle segmentation   Separating consumers into groups based
on their hobbies, interests, and other personal choices.

linage   Refers to the size of an ad, based on the number of lines of
type it takes up.

local advertising   (1) Advertising to a local merchant or business
as opposed to regional or national target. (2) Advertising placed
at rates available to local merchants.

local rate   An advertising rate charged to a local advertiser,
typically a retailer, by local media and publications, as
distinguished from a national rate that is charged to a national
advertiser, typically a manufacturer.

logotype (logo)   A brand or company name presented in a special
lettering style or typeface and used in the manner of a trademark.

loss leader   A retail item advertised at an invitingly low price
in order to attract customers for the purchase of other, more
profitable merchandise.

loyalty index   A broadcast station's frequency of people who tune
in to it.

mail order advertising   Advertising that supplies ordering forms
for the purpose of soliciting a purchase made through the mail.

make good   (1) To present a commercial announcement after its
scheduled time because of an error. (2) To rerun a commercial

announcement because of technical difficulties the previous time it was run. (3) To rerun a print advertisement due to similar circumstances.

marginal analysis Technique of setting the advertising budget by assuming the point at which an additional dollar spent on advertising equals additional profit.

marketing mix The levels and interplay of the elements of a product's or service's marketing efforts, including product features, pricing, packaging, advertising, merchandising, distribution, and marketing budget.

marketing research The systematic gathering, recording, analyzing, and use of data relating to the transfer and sale of goods and services from producer to consumer.

market profile A summary of the characteristics of a market, including information on typical purchasers and competitors; and, often, general information on the economy and retailing patterns of an area.

market segmentation To divide a market by a strategy directed at gaining a major portion of sales by a subgroup in a category, rather than a more limited share of purchases by all category users.

market share The percentage of a product category's sales, in terms of dollars or units, obtained by a brand, line, or company.

materiality The FTC theoretically will not regulate a deceptive advertisement unless the deceptive claim is also material. This means that the claim must be important to consumers. Specifically, the FTC requires that the deception be likely to affect consumers' "choice of, or conduct regarding, a product."

media concentration theory Technique of scheduling media that involves buying space in one medium only and developing strength through concentration.

media dominance theory Technique of scheduling media that involves buying a large amount of space in one medium, and shifting to another medium after achieving optimum coverage and frequency.

media plan Designed to select the proper demographics for an advertising campaign through proper media selection.

media strategy A plan of action by an advertiser for bringing advertising messages to the attention of consumers through the use of appropriate media.

merchandising the advertising The promoting of a firm's advertising abilities to distributors.

milline rate   Used to determine the cost effectiveness of advertising in a newspaper. The rate is calculated by multiplying the cost per agate line by one million, then dividing by the circulation. Also referred to as milline.

motivation research   Used to investigate the psychological reasons why individuals buy specific types of merchandise, or why they respond to specific advertising appeals, to determine the base of brand choices and product preferences.

NAD   National Advertising Division of the Council of Better Business Bureaus. This organization serves as a major self-regulatory mechanism for advertising.

NARB   National Advertising Review Board of the Council of Better Business Bureaus. When an alleged problem arises with an advertisement and a satisfactory solution is not obtained via the **NAD**, the NARB acts in the capacity of an appeals board. It reviews the decision of the NAD and passes judgment on it.

narrowcasting   Using a broadcast medium to appeal to audiences with special interests. For example, the "All-Knitting Station" would be a narrowcast.

national brand   A nationally distributed product brand name. May also be distributed regionally or locally.

net cost   The costs associated with services rendered by an advertising agency excluding the agency commission.

net unduplicated audience   The combined cumulative audience exposed to an advertisement.

Nielsen rating   A measurement of the percentage of U.S. television households tuned to a network program for a minute of its telecast.

noncommercial advertising   Radio and television advertising that is designed to educate and promote ideas or institutions. Also called public service announcements.

O & O station   Radio and television stations owned and operated by a network.

off card   Advertising time sold at a rate that does not appear on the rate card.

on-air tests   Determining recall among viewers of a commercial or program during a real broadcast of the communication.

opticals   Visual effects used to instill interest as well as portray mood and continuity in a commercial. Dissolves, cross fades, and montages are all opticals.

outdoor advertising   Any outdoor sign that publicly promotes a product or service, such as billboards and movie kiosks.

▼

package A combination of programs or commercials offered by a network that is available for purchase by advertisers either singly or as a discounted deal.

package insert Separate material included in merchandise packages that advertises goods or services. Also referred to as package stuffer.

painted bulletin A freestanding steel or wooden structure, approximately 50 feet wide by 15 feet high, with molding around the outer edges similar to a poster panel, and including a hand-painted copy message. Bulletins are generally found near highways or roofs of buildings in high traffic areas.

Pantone Matching System (PMS) A set of color chips that characterizes a color so that it can be matched, even by different printers. By knowing the Pantone color specifications, a printer does not even need to see a sample of the color in order to match it.

parity products Several brands within a category that possess functionally equivalent attributes, making one brand a satisfactory substitute for most others in that category.

pass-along readers A reader who becomes familiar with a publication without purchasing it. These readers are taken into account when calculating the publication's total number of readers.

paste-up A camera-ready layout of illustrative and type material that is configured in the proper position on paperboard and is used for reproductive purposes.

payout planning Approach to advertising budgeting in which the dollars spent to advertise are represented as an investment toward sales and profits.

percent-of-sales method Determining the advertising budget based on an analysis of past sales, as well as a forecast for future sales.

per inquiry An agreement between a media representative and an advertiser in which all advertising fees are paid based on a percentage of all money received from sales or inquires.

persons using television (PUT) A percentage of all persons in a certain viewing area that are viewing television during a specific amount of time. Used by A.C. Nielson.

persons viewing television (PVT) Same meaning as above, except this term is used by Arbitron.

persuasion process The process used by advertising to influence audience or prospect attitudes, especially purchase intent and product perception, by appealing to reason or emotion.

photoboards A set of still photographs made from a television commercial, accompanied with a script, to be kept as records by an agency or client.

photostat A type of high-contrast photographic negative or positive in the form of paper. Also referred to as a "stat."

picture window An ad layout in which the picture is placed at the top of the page, and the copy is placed below.

piggyback (1) A direct mail offer that is included free with another offer. (2) Two commercials which are shown back-to-back by the same sponsor.

point-of-purchase (POP) displays Advertising display material located at the retail store, usually placed near the checkout counter.

poster panel An outdoor billboard displaying ads printed on paper sheets rather than being painted. The most widely used form of outdoor advertising; standard size approximately 25 feet x 12 feet with the image printed on sections of 24 to 30 sheets.

post testing Testing the effects of an ad after it has appeared in the media.

preemptible rate A usually discounted rate for commercial time, which is sold to an advertiser and is not guaranteed. Time may be sold to another advertiser who is willing to pay more; therefore, the advertiser buying this rate gambles to save money on the spot.

preferred position A position in a printed publication that is thought to attract the most reader attention and is sold at a higher rate. For example, the back cover of a magazine.

preprint A reproduction of an advertisement that is viewed before actual publication and is created by an advertiser for special purposes, such as to serve as retail displays or to gain support from retailers.

pretesting Testing an advertisement or an audience sample prior to placing the ad in the media.

prime time The broadcast periods viewed or listened to by the greatest number of persons and for which a station charges the most for air time. In television, the hours are usually 8:00 P.M. to 11:00 P.M. E.S.T. (7:00 P.M. to 10:00 P.M. C.S.T.).

Problem
Solving

Attack Ads

When the going gets tough, the tough get going. That old locker-room adage could just as well apply to advertising, judging from the rise in aggressive attacks ads during the economic downturn in 2009.

Some of the face-offs in these so-called attack ads have included Campbell Soup vs. Progresso, Domino's vs. Subway, and Dunkin' Donuts vs. Starbucks, according to Emily Bryson York in "The Gloves Are Off: More Marketers Opt for Attack Ads," Adage.com. "While comparative advertising can boost sales when done well," York writes, "you risk getting sued or alienating consumers when you go after a rival."

In its sub sandwich ads, Domino's claimed its subs had beaten Subway in a national taste test. When Subway responded with a cease-and-desist letter, Domino's president burned the letter in a TV spot. PR got in on the action when Domino's even issued a press release asking, "Did you know Domino's was in a food fight?" The company claimed victory: During the quarter when the ads ran, it reported a 1 percent same-store-sales gain for the quarter, the first positive result in the domestic business for some time.

Tim Calkins, a marketing professor at Northwestern University's Kellogg School of Business, acknowledges that comparative

private brand Product brand owned by a retailer, wholesaler, dealer, or merchant, as opposed to a manufacturer or producer, and bearing its own company name or another name it owns exclusively. Also referred to as **private label**.

product differentiation Developing unique product differences with the intent of influencing demand.

product life cycle A marketing theory concerning a product's sequence of stages including: introduction, growth, maturity, and sales decline.

product management Assigning specific products or brands to be managed by single managers within an advertising agency.

advertising can be an effective way to differentiate a product, York reports. But he says that the key question is whether advertisers get more for their dollar by promoting their brand's attributes or taking on a competitor—especially since many attack ads result in litigation.

In 2009, for example, Sara Lee sued Kraft over claims that Kraft's Oscar Mayer's franks beat Sara Lee's Ball Park in a taste test, York states. Sara Lee complained that Kraft used Ball Park Beef Franks to conduct the taste test, but the ad copy implied that Oscar Mayer beat the entire Ball Park product line, which also includes cheese franks and turkey franks.

Before going after a competitor, York says, advertisers can avoid such legal battles by considering the following guidelines:

Don't name your competitor—Claims naming vague targets such as "some of our competitors" are a lot less likely to be challenged in court.

Stay positive—Tout a positive attribute such as "tastes better" rather than a potentially off-putting claim like "less fatty." A negative description can drive down sales in an entire product category.

Support claims with science—If a claim sounds questionable, savvy consumers will question your comparison.

Have a back-up ad—If a competitor's response causes you to pull your spot, you'll still be able to use your airtime.

product placement Integrating an advertiser's product into noncommercial content such as television programs, feature films, radio programs, or news articles.

product positioning The way advertisers want consumers to perceive a product or service as compared to its competition.

program delivery (rate) Percentage of a sample group of people tuned in to a particular program at a particular time.

promotion All forms of communication other than advertising that call attention to products and services by adding extra value for their purchase. Includes temporary discounts, allowances, premium offers, coupons, contests, and sweepstakes.

promotional mix   Using several different types of communication for marketing goals, including advertising, personal selling, publicity, and sales promotions.

proof   A preliminary stage of an ad produced on paper, for the purpose of checking the correctness and quality before it is printed.

psychographics   Describing consumers or audience members on the basis of psychological characteristics initially determined by standardized tests.

publicity   A type of public relations in the form of a news item or story about a product, service, or idea in the media.

public relations (PR)   Communication with various sectors of the public to influence their attitudes and opinions about a person, product, or idea.

public service advertising (PSA)   Advertising with a central focus on public welfare, generally sponsored by a non-profit institution, civic group, religious organization, trade association, or political group.

puffery   A legal term for the exaggeration of praise lavished on a product that stops just short of deception.

pulsing   The use of advertising in regular intervals, as opposed to seasonal patterns.

pupilometrics   A method of advertising research that studies the relationship between a viewer's pupil dilation and his interest in visual stimuli.

psychological segmentation   The grouping of consumers into psychological characteristic categories on the basis of standardized tests.

qualitative research   A method of advertising research focused on meaning in consumer perceptions and attitudes; for example, in-depth interviews and focus groups.

quantitative research   A method of advertising research that emphasizes measuring the incidence of consumer trends within a population.

rate   (1) The amount charged by a communications medium to an advertiser based on per unit of space or time purchased. The rate may vary from national to local campaigns, or may be a fixed rate. (2) To estimate a particular media's audience size based on a research sample.

rate card   Cards from both print and broadcast media containing information about advertising costs, mechanical requirements, issue dates, closing dates, cancellation dates, and circulation data.

rating point   (1) In television, one percentage of all TV households who are viewing a particular station at a given time. (2) In radio, 1 percent of all listeners who are listening to a particular station at a given time. Both instances vary depending on time of day.

reach   The estimated number of individuals in the audience of broadcast or outdoor-advertising media that is reached at least once during a specific period of time.

readership   (1) The total number of readers of a publication. (2) The percentage of people who can recall a particular advertisement, aided or unaided.

recognition   (1) A communications medium formal acknowledgment an advertising agency as being bona fide, competent, and ethical, and therefore entitled to discounts. (2) The ability of research subjects to recall a particular ad or campaign when they see or hear it.

rep or representative   A person who solicits advertising space on behalf of a particular medium.

residuals   A sum paid to a performer on a TV or radio commercial each time it is run, usually established by an AFTRA (American Federation of Television and Radio Artists) or SAG (Screen Actors Guild) contract.

retail advertising   Advertising that promotes local merchandisers' goods and services. Also referred to as local advertising.

retail trading zone   Defined by the Audit Bureau of Circulation as the area beyond an urban area whose residents regularly trade with retail merchants within the urban area.

road block   A method of scheduling broadcast commercials to obtain maximum reach by simultaneously showing the identical advertisement on several different stations.

run-of-press (ROP)   A newspaper publisher's option to place an ad anywhere in the publication that they choose, as opposed to preferred position. Also referred to as run-of-paper.

run-of-schedule (ROS)   A station's option to place a commercial in any time slot that they choose.

sales promotion   Marketing activities that stimulate consumer purchasing and dealer effectiveness through a combination of personal selling, advertising, and all supplementary selling activities.

scene setting   Using realistic sounds to stimulate noise in backgrounds during radio production such as car horns, sirens, and recorded laughter, etc.

selective distribution   Manufacturers' option to distribute their products only to those wholesalers and retailers who follow their guidelines, so they can maintain more control over the way their products are sold and discourage price competition.

sets in use (SIU)   The percent of television sets that are tuned into a particular broadcast during a specific amount of time.

share-of-audience   The percent of audiences that are tuned into a particular medium at a given time, such as the number of people watching television between the hours of 8:00 P.M. to 11:00 P.M.

share-of-voice (SOV)   The total percentage that an advertiser possesses of the particular niche, market, or audience it is targeting.

Simmons Market Research Bureau (SMRB)   A syndicated service that provides audience exposure and product-usage data for print and broadcast media.

situation analysis   The gathering and evaluation of information to identify the target group and strategic direction of an advertising campaign.

speculative (spec) sample   A sample promotional product, with the prospective buyer's imprint on it, produced with the hope that the customer will purchase it.

split run   Two or more different forms of an advertisement placed simultaneously in different copies of the same publication to test the effectiveness of one ad over another.

spread   A pair of facing pages in a periodical, or an advertisement that is printed across two such pages.

staggered schedule   A schedule of advertisements in a number of periodicals that have different insertion dates.

Standard Advertising Unit System (SAUS)   A set of uniform advertising procedures developed by the American Newspaper Publishers Association.

Standard Rate and Data Service (SRDS)   A commercial firm that publishes reference volumes that include up-to-date information on rates, requirements, closing dates, and other information necessary for ad placement in the media.

Starch scores   A result of a method used by Daniel Starch and staff in their studies of advertising readership. Categories of scores include: noted, or the percent of readers who viewed the tested ad; associated, or the percent of readers who associated the ad with the advertiser; and read-most, or the percent of readers who read half or more of the copy.

stet   A Latin term meaning "let it stand," which instructs a printer or typesetter to ignore an alteration called for in a proof.

storyboard   A blueprint for a TV commercial that is drawn to portray copy, dialogue, and action, with caption notes regarding filming, audio components, and script.

subliminal persuasion   An advertising message presented below the threshold of consciousness. A visual or auditory message that is allegedly perceived psychologically, but not consciously.

superimposition (super)   A process in TV production where an image, words, or phrases are imposed over another image.

supplementary media   Non-mass media vehicles that are used to promote products, such as point-of-purchase advertising.

swatch proof   A sample of the material for a promotional product, with the customer's artwork printed on it in the specified colors.

sweeps   A time during the months of November, March, and May when both Nielson and Arbitron survey all local market broadcast media for the purpose of rating the stations and their programming.

syndicated program   A television or radio program that is distributed in more than one market by an organization other than a network.

tabloid   A size of newspaper that is roughly half the size of a standard newspaper. A page size is normally 14 inches high by 12 inches wide.

tachistoscope testing   Measure a viewer's recognition and perception of various elements within an ad by using the different lighting and exposure techniques of a tachistoscope—a device that projects an image at a fraction of a second.

tag line   A slogan or phrase that conveys the most important product attribute or benefit that the advertiser wishes to convey. Generally, the theme of a campaign.

target audience   A specified audience or demographic group for which an advertising message is designed.

tear sheets   A page cut from a magazine or newspaper that is sent to the advertiser as proof of the ad insertion. Also used to check color reproduction of advertisements.

thumbnail   A rough, simple, often small sketch used to show the basic layout of an ad.

trade advertising   Advertising designed to increase sales specifically for retailers and wholesalers.

trademark   Icon, symbol, or brand name used to identify a specific manufacturer, product, or service.

typeface   A designed alphabet for printing with consistent characteristics and attributes.

type font   Refers to the complete alphabet for a specific typeface.

unaided recall   A research method in which a respondent is given no assistance in answering questions regarding a specific advertisement.

unfair advertising   Advertising that is likely to harm the consumer. The FTC has the power to regulate unfair advertising that falls within a very specific legal definition.

unique selling proposition (USP)   The unique product benefit that the competition cannot claim.

upfront buys   The purchasing of both broadcast and print early in the buying season.

values and lifestyles (VALS) research   A research method that groups consumers based on certain characteristics such as their values, lifestyles, and demographics.

vehicle   A specific channel or publication for carrying the advertising message to a target audience. For example, one medium would be magazines, while one vehicle would be *Time* magazine.

vertical publications   Publications with editorial content addressed to the interests of a specific industry, such as *National Petroleum Magazine* and *Retail Baking Today*.

vignette   (1) An illustration that has soft edges, often produced by using cutouts or masks. (2) A photograph or halftone in which the edges, or parts of them, are shaded off to a very light gray.

viral marketing   Techniques that try to exploit exiting social networks to create an exponential increase in brand awareness.

voice-pitch analysis (VOPAN)   Analyzing a subject's voice during their responses to test their feelings and attitudes about an ad.

voiceover (VO)   The technique of using the voice of an unseen speaker during a film, slides, or a video.

waste circulation   (1) Advertising in an area where the product or service is not available or has no sales potential. (2) Persons in an advertiser's audience who are not potential consumers.

wave scheduling   Scheduling space in the media in intermittent periods, such as two weeks on, two weeks off.

wear out   The point reached when an advertising campaign loses its effectiveness due to repeated play of ads.

weight   (1) An adjustment made in a survey sample to correct for demographic or geographic imbalances. (2) Number of exposures of an advertisement.

Sources: University of Texas Advertising and Public Relations, (http://advertising.utexas.edu/PublicRelations); Adglossary.com; *Advertising Is Dead, Long Live Advertising.* By Tim Himpe (Thames, & Hudson, 2006)

Chapter 6

Resources

Associations and Organizations

Adhouse New York, New York Instead of the traditional, preset, multiple-course structure, Adhouse creates "prescriptive programs" for creatives at all stages of their careers. A selection of 10-week classes takes students through the process of portfolio development. Or Students can take courses a la carte. (http://www.adhousenyc.com)

Berlin School of Creative Leadership at Steinbeis University Berlin, Germany "Turning great creatives into great creative leaders" is the mission of the newly founded Berlin School. With a broader scope than the typical advertising graduate program, the school aims to foster global discourse on creative leadership in media, entertainment, advertising, design, journalism, and marketing. Its Executive MBA in Creative Leadership is a part-time program spread over one year, taking place in Berlin and other creative industry hotspots like Chicago, New York, London, Shanghai, and Tokyo. (http://www.berlin-school.com)

VCU Brandcenter, Richmond, Virginia Founded in 1996 as the VCU Adcenter, VCU Brandcenter was the first graduate program in marketing communications to combine the business of brand management with a creative program for art directors, writers, and technologists in an agency setting. The school's goal is to "transform the business of advertising and branding by training the next generation of leaders to make the business smarter, less

On the Cutting Edge

Webcasts Market Surgery

Online advertising and health care have both seen dramatic technological advances over the past few years. Now they are teaming up to market a service that has previously been considered to be very private: surgery, according to Pam Belluck in her article "Webcast Your Brain Surgery? Hospitals See Marketing Tool," published on Mytimes.com.

Case in point: In 2009, Methodist University Hospital in Memphis broadcast a video Webcast of a patient's awake craniotomy, in which the patient remains conscious and talking while surgeons prod and cut inside the brain. The brain surgery was performed to remove a malignant tumor threatening to paralyze the patient's left side.

The hospital's marketing department saw the broadcast as a way of boosting their reputation and educating the community. But some ethicists and physicians say the practice raises questions about patient privacy and could present an overly optimistic picture of complicated procedures, Belluck writes.

The ubiquitous device Twitter has also found its way into the operating room. At Henry Ford Hospital in Detroit, the device has been used during an operation to remove a kidney tumor, a hysterectomy and a craniotomy, during which the hospital posted video on YouTube.

What if something goes wrong during surgery? Methodist Hospital records an identical surgery on another patient, Belluck points out, so if the camera has to cut away from surgery that's underway they can switch to the previous surgery. On this point E. Haavi Morreim, an ethicist at the University of Tennessee College of Medicine, is quoted as saying, "If you don't show the bad along with the good, people can end up misinformed or with excessively optimistic expectations."

Despite the potential problems, more than 250 hospitals now use YouTube, Facebook, Twitter, or blogs, according to one medical Web strategy director. Like other types of marketing campaigns, online health care broadcasts have produced some unexpected results, Belluck reports. After Methodist advertised a coming brain-surgery Webcast, a man volunteered to be the patient. As an example of "the halo effect," the brain-surgery broadcasts have brought patients to the hospital's other departments.

conventional and more responsible." It has been ranked one of top digital-media schools in country. (http://www.brandcenter.vcu.edu)

Books and Periodicals

Books

Adcult USA: The Triumph of Advertising in American Culture. By James B. Twitchell (Columbia University Press, 1996). Details the effects of advertising on American culture.

The Adman in the Parlor: Magazines and the Gendering of Consumer Culture, 1880s to 1910s. By Ellen Gruber Garvey (Oxford University Press, 1996). Discusses the beginning of consumerism in the United States.

The Ad Men and Women: A Biographical Dictionary of Advertising. By Edd Applegate (Greenwood Press, 1994). Profiles 54 influential men and women in advertising.

Adventures of an Advertising Woman. By Jane Maas (Ballantine Books, 1986). Memoir by one of the first women to become an ad executive.

Advertising, Alcohol Consumption, and Mortality: An Empirical Investigation. By Joseph C. Fisher and Peter A. Cook (Greenwood Press, 1995). Challenges an earlier study showing advertising had little impact on drinking.

Advertising and a Democratic Press. By C. Edwin Baker (Princeton University Press, 1994). The impact of the media's dependence on advertising.

Advertising and Marketing to the New Majority. By Gail Baker Woods (Wadsworth Publishing Co., 1995). Advertising's effects on ethnic audiences.

Advertising and Popular Culture. By Jib Fowles (Sage Publications, 1996). How advertising both draws from and contributes to popular culture.

Advertising and the Mind of the Consumer (2nd Ed.). By Max Sutherland and Alice K. Sylvester (Allen & Unwin, 2000). Psychological perspective on how ads work.

Advertising and the Transformation of American Society, 1865-1920. By James D. Norris (Greenwood Press, 1990). How the United States became a consumer society.

The Advertising Controversy. By Mark S. Albion and Paul Farris

(Auburn House, 1981). Evaluates conflicting claims about advertising's economic effects.

Advertising Copywriting. By Philip W. Burton (Grid Publishers, 1978). Comprehensive guide covers writing from local campaigns to national TV ads.

Advertising Creativity: Techniques for Generating Ideas. By James L. Marra (Prentice-Hall, 1990). Approaches creativity as the ability to think by making connections.

Advertising in America: the First 200 Years. By Charles A. Goodrum and Helen Dalrymple (Harry N. Abrams, 1990). An encyclopedia of the print advertising image and ideas about why advertising has flourished.

Advertising Media Planning. By Jack Z. Sissors and Jim Surmanek (Crain Books, 1976). This popular text teaches the fundamentals of planning, purchasing, and evaluating the effectiveness of advertising.

Advertising Progress: American Business and the Rise of Consumer Marketing. By Pamela Walker Laird (The Johns Hopkins University Press, 1998). Thoroughly illustrated account of early consumerism.

Advertising Today. By Warren Berger (Phaidon Press, 2001). A thematic overview of the evolution of advertising around the world over the past 30 years.

Agency Compensation: A Guidebook (2nd Ed.). By Stanley Beals and David Beals (Association of National Advertisers, Inc., 2001). Concise volume analyzes many compensation issues.

The Age of Propaganda: The Everyday Use and Abuse of Persuasion. By Anthony Pratkanis and Elliot Aronson (W. H. Freeman, 2000). Social psychologists' perspective on mass persuasion.

Are They Selling Her Lips? Advertising and Identity. By Carole Moog (William Morrow and Company, 1990). How ads affect self-image.

The Art of Writing Advertising: Conversations with Masters of the Craft. By Dennis Higgins (NTC Business Books, 1987). A discussion among five masters of the craft.

Attitudes and Persuasion. By Richard E. Petty and John T. Cacioppo (Westview Press, 1995). Theoretical approaches to changing attitudes and beliefs.

Aunt Jemima, Uncle Ben, and Rastus: Blacks in Advertising, Yesterday, Today, and Tomorrow. By Richard E.Marilyn Kern-Foxworth

Professional
Ethics

Deceptive Advertising

As part of its Resources section, the Web site for Texas Advertising at The University of Texas at Austin (http://advertising.utexas.edu) includes the article "Deception," by Jef I. Richards. The article's discussion of government regulation is summarized here:

Since 1914, the Federal Trade Commission (FTC) has been the primary regulator of deceptive advertising in the U.S. The Wheeler-Lea Amendment to the act that created the Commission later gave it the authority over both "unfair methods of competition" and "unfair or deceptive acts or practices." It is through this authority that the FTC regulates deceptive advertising. The Commission publishes advertising guidelines for marketers, which are not law but merely advisory, and adopts trade-regulation rules, which are law.

The FTC considers an advertisement to be deceptive if "there is a representation, omission, act or practice that...is likely to mislead consumers acting reasonably under the circumstances, and... if that representation, omission, or practice is 'material.'" The term "material" refers to deceptions that affect consumers' "choice of, or conduct regarding, a product."

In determining whether an ad claim is deceptive, the FTC is not generally concerned with what it says, but what it conveys to consumers. If the conveyed message differs from the actual product attribute being advertised, the claim is considered deceptive. This judgment requires the Commission to consider two types of

(Greenwood Press, 1994). Representations of African Americans in advertising from the 19th century to the present.

A Big Life in Advertising. By Mary Wells Lawrence (Alfred A. Knopf, 2002). Insider's look at 30 years of the ad business and her breaking into a man's world.

Bill Bernbach's Book : a History of the Advertising That Changed the History of Advertising. By Bob Levenson (Villard Books, 1987). Deluxe, illustrated chronicle of the leader of the Creative Revolution.

evidence: the message that is conveyed to consumers and the product attribute's true qualities.

The FTC considers surveys the best way to determine what message is conveyed by an ad, though sometimes the Commission relies on other evidence. The murky issue of uncovering consumers' thoughts has been the subject of considerable research and discussion.

Several methods are used to assess a product's attributes. For an automobile's fuel mileage, for example, laboratory testing of the vehicle's fuel efficiency would normally be undertaken. However, the FTC requires that advertisers conduct such testing prior to making the ad claim. If a claim is made without evidence in hand that the product will perform as advertised, known as "substantiation," the claim will be considered deceptive.

Most cases started by the FTC never require the Commission to make a final decision about the advertiser's deceptiveness. Those cases end in a "consent order," whereby the advertiser agrees to do what the FTC asks. In those cases that do end in a final FTC decision finding the claim deceptive, the advertiser will face one of three possible remedies: "(1) a Cease and Desist Order, which requires the advertiser to stop making the claim, (2) an Affirmative Disclosure Order, which forces the advertiser to provide consumers with more information, or (3) Corrective Advertising, which is a form of affirmative disclosure that is intended to correct lingering deception that results from a long history of deceiving the consumer."

Blood, Brains & Beer: The Autobiography of David Ogilvy. By David Ogilvy (Atheneum, 1978). The colorful life of an industry giant.

The Brothers: The Saatchi & Saatchi Story. By Ivan Fallon (Contemporary Books, 1989). Chronicle of the 1980's dynamic duo of the ad world.

Build a Better Financial Relationship with your Agencies. By Joanne Davis, with Joel Kushins (Association of National Advertisers, Inc., 2003). Booklet covers defining expectations and managing media, fee, and production audits.

Can't Buy My Love: How Advertising Changes the Way We Think and Feel. By Jean Kilbourne (Simon & Schuster, 1999). A critique of advertising's powerful influence.

Captains of Consciousness. By Stuart Ewen (McGraw-Hill Book Company, 1976). Analysis of the ad industry at the turn of the 20th century.

The Care and Feeding of Ideas. By Bill Backer (Times Books [Random House], 1993). Explains the creative process and how to use it.

Channels of Desire: Mass Images and the Shaping of American Consciousness. By Stuart Ewen and Elizabeth Ewen (University of Minnesota Press, 1992). Documents the power of images.

Chiat/Day: The First Twenty Years. By Stephen Kessler (Rizzoli, 1990). A history of this influential agency.

The Commercialization of American Culture: New Advertising, Control and Democracy. By Matthew P. McAllister (Sage Publications, 1996). Considers ad techniques introduced in the 1990s, such as niche marketing, database marketing, and place-based marketing.

Communications of An Advertising Man. By Leo Burnett (University of Chicago Press, 1961). A selection from the ad legend's speeches, articles, and other writings.

Confessions of an Ad Man. By David Ogilvy (Atheneum, 1963). The first complete statement of the highly influential adman's take on the business.

The Copywriter's Handbook : A Step-by-Step Guide To Writing That Sells. By Robert W. Bly (Henry Holt, 1990). Though it predates the Internet, the book's advice is still considered relevant and helpful.

Creating Effective Advertising Using Semiotics. By Mihai Nadin and Richard D. Zakia (The Consultant Press, Ltd., 1994). Using the science of signs to create visual advertising.

Creative Leaps: 10 Lessons in Effective Advertising Inspired at Saatchi & Saatchi. By Michael Newman (John Wiley & Sons, 2003). The strategies, creative thinking, and stories behind some of the agency's most successful campaigns.

The Day the Pigs Refused to Be Driven to Market. By Robin Wight (MacGibbon Ltd., 1972). An early work on consumer education.

Decoding Advertisements. By Judith Williamson (Marion Boyers, 1978). A key text on media studies for the general audience.

Disruption: Overturning Conventions and Shaking Up the Marketplace. By Jean-Marie Dru (John Wiley & Sons, 1996). Uncovering the biases and conventions in business thinking in order to promote clear, creative thinking.

Effective Advertising: Understanding When, How, and Why Advertising Works. By Gerard J. Tellis (Sage Publications, 2004). Reviews and summarizes 50 years of research on what makes ads work.

The Elements of Style (4th Ed.). By William Strunk and E. B. White (Longman, 2000). Essential guide to clear, concise writing.

Emperors of Adland: Inside the Advertising Revolution. By Nancy Millman (Warner Books, 1988). Discusses the major agency mergers of the 1980s.

The End Of Advertising As We Know It. By Sergio Zyman (John Wiley & Sons, 2002). Views advertising as everything from packaging to employee behavior and states that advertising must show a measurable return.

The Erotic History of Advertising. By Tom Reichert (Prometheus Books, 2003). Amply illustrated study of the use of sex in 20th-century ads.

Evaluating Agency Performance. By Stanley Beals (Association of National Advertisers, Inc., 2003). Best practices for assessing an ad's effectiveness.

Fables of Abundance: A Cultural History of Advertising in America. By Jackson Lears (BasicBooks, 1994). Documents the changing nature of advertising up to the period when television was introduced.

The Fall of Advertising and the Rise of PR. By Al Ries and Laura Ries (2002). New York: HarperBusiness. Champions public relations as the best way to promote brands.

5 Giants of Advertising. By Philippe Lorin with Cristina Alonso (Assouline Publishing, 2001). History of the business told through the careers of a handful of its stars.

From Those Wonderful Folks Who Gave Your Pearl Harbor. By Jerry Della Famina (Pocket Books, 1971). An insider's humorous account of the business.

George, Be Careful. By George Lois and Bill Pitts (Saturday Review Press, 1972). Lowdown on the ad industry by an innovative iconoclast.

Going Negative: How Attack Ads Shrink and Polarize the Electorate. By Stephen Ansolabehere and Shanto Iyengar (Free Press, 1995). A six-year study of political advertising.

Great Print Advertising: Creative Approaches, Strategies, and Tactics. By Tony Antin (John Wiley & Sons, 1993). A wealth of examples is used to identify the hallmarks of the top print ads.

Harvesting Minds: How TV Commercials Control Kids. By Roy F. Fox (Praeger, 1996). Collects and analyzes children's comments on Channel One advertising.

Hey Whipple, Squeeze This: A Guide to Creating Great Ads. By Sullivan Luke (John Wiley & Sons, 1998; revised edition in 2003). An accomplished copywriter uses his skills to inspire the creation of engaging, intelligent ads.

The Hidden Persuaders. By Vance Packard (McKay, 1957). A landmark book on the influence of advertising on daily life.

A History of Advertising from the Earliest Times. By Henry Sampson (Chatto and Windus, 1874). From the first British newspapers to colonial American ads.

How to Advertise. By Kenneth Roman and Jane Maas (St. Martins Press, 1976). A classic text revised (third edition) to include interactive media.

How to Become an Advertising Man. By James Webb Young (NTC Business Books, 1989). Provides seven core concepts pertaining to the profession.

How to Put Your Book Together and Get a Job in Advertising. By Maxine Paetro (The Copy Workshop, 1990). Assembling a portfolio and other career advice from a number of well-known ad pros.

How to Write Advertising That Sells. By Clyde Bedell (McGraw-Hill Book Company, 1952). Provides 31 strategies for improving copy.

How to Write a Good Advertisement. By Victor Schwab (Harper, 1962). Copywriting basics presented largely through the study of headlines.

In Defense of Advertising: Arguments from Reason, Ethical Egoism, and Laissez-Faire Capitalism. By Jerry Kirkpatrick (Quorum Books, 1994). The role of advertising in a free-market economy.

Inventing Desire: Inside Chiat/Day, the Hottest Shop, the Coolest Players, the Big Business of Advertising. By Karen Stabiner (Simon & Schuster, 1993). A candid look at the agency told in narrative form.

Is There Any Hope for Advertising? By Howard Luck Gossage (University of Illinois Press, 1986). Irreverent look at advertising from a star of the Sixties and Seventies.

John Caples: Adman. By Gordon White (Crain Books, 1977). Biography of the legendary copywriter.

Kids as Consumers: A Handbook of Marketing to Children. By James

U. McNeal (Lexington Books, 1992). A thorough study of this young market.

The Lasker Story: As He Told It. By Albert Lasker (NTC Business Books, 1987). A memoir by the man who was head of the Lord and Thomas agency in the early 20th century.

Leo Burnett: Star Reacher. By Joan Kufrin (Leo Burnett Company, Inc., 1995). Biography of the famous advertising man who encouraged colleagues to reach for the stars.

Lovemarks: the Future Beyond Brand. By Kevin Roberts (PowerHouse Books, 2004). A Saatchi & Saatchi executive gives his views on brands and consumer loyalty.

Madison Avenue USA. By Martin Mayer (Pocketbooks, 1958). A classic account of the ad business at mid-century.

Marion Harper: An Unauthorized Biography. By Russ Johnston (Crain Books, 1982). Story of one the founders of the successful Needham Harper & Steers agency.

Marketing to the Mind: Right Brain Strategies for Advertising and Marketing. By Richard C. Maddock and Richard L. Fulton (Quorum Books, 1996). A psychologist's views on consumer motivation and behavior.

Measuring Advertising Effectiveness. Edited by William D. Wells (Lawrence Erlbaum, 1997). Explores the multidimensional nature of advertising's effects from both academic and applied perspectives.

Measuring the Effectiveness of Image and Linkage Advertising: The Nitty-Gritty of Maxi-Marketing. By Arch G. Woodside (Quorum Books, 1996). Provides a 20-step model of how certain types of advertising work and shows how to assess advertising impact.

Media Sexploitation. By Wilson Bryan Key (Prentice-Hall, Inc., 1976). Present's the author's views on subliminal advertising.

The Mirror Makers. By Stephen Fox (Vintage Books, 1984). Industry history told through the contributions of key players.

My Life in Advertising. By Claude C. Hopkins (Crain Books, 1976). Biography of one the fathers of direct marketing.

Ogilvy on Advertising. By David Ogilvy (Crown Publishers, 1983). One of the "bibles" of copywriters and art directors.

The Persuasion Handbook. By Dillard, James P. & Michael Pfau (Sage Publications, 2002). Explains what it means to be "persuaded."

Persuasion: Theory and Research. By Daniel J. O'Keefe, (Sage Publications, 2002). A comprehensive and critical treatment of theory and research in persuasion.

On the Cutting
Edge

Interactive Print Ads

A button on a Yellow Tail wine ad sets off four blinking firefly tails. *Maxim* magazine and Lionsgate Home Entertainment create a "rip proof" synthetic paper page promoting the DVD of the tough-guy film *The Condemned*. An Aquafina sparkling water ad has a bottle-shaped piece of bubble wrap in the magazine issue in which it appears.

Once the province of Web advertising, interactive advertisements like these are now being placed in magazine pages, according to Laura Petrecca in her article "New, 'interactive' print ads fight for your attention," on USAToday.com (http://www.usatoday.com). Marketers are taking advantage of smaller, less expensive audio chips and batteries to bring added dimensions to print ads.

Their motivation is a familiar one in advertising: to try to stand out amid ad clutter. Petrecca quotes a magazine publisher who says the average American adult is exposed to roughly 3,000 advertising or brand messages a day—underscoring the importance of standing out.

Interactive print ads are likely to become more popular, as research has found that readers remember "spectacular" print ads. For instance, 96 percent of readers remembered seeing an ad for Clairol Herbal Essences with the conditioner Hawafena; the ad played a song "Haw-a-fena" (to the tune of Handel's "Hallelujah" chorus), Petrecca reports.

The new ads have to do more than just engage the readers' senses, of course. They still have to convey the brand's message, making the creative execution as important as ever.

Some recent examples of print-ad creativity that Petrecca cites:

To promote mobile-service provider Helio, ad agency Deutsch LA produced a booklet about communicating in a digital world. The insert has run in publications such as *GQ*, *Spin*, and *Allure*.

To promote the new show *Cane*, about a family-run rum business, CBS worked with marketing agency Initiative to place rum-flavored "taste strips" in a magazine.

Diet Pepsi Jazz's pop-up ad not only had a scratch-and-sniff tab that emitted a black-cherry and French vanilla scent, it also played a jazzy tune when opened. Media agency OMD placed it in select markets in *People*.

Persuasive Communication. By James B. Stiff and Paul A. Mongeau (Guilford Press, 2003). This textbook is a synthesis of persuasion literature.

Please Be Ad-vised: The Legal Reference Guide for the Advertising Executive (4th Ed.). By Douglas J. Wood (Association of National Advertisers, Inc., 2003). A practical tool for avoiding legal problems.

The Power of Persuasion. By Robert Levine (John Wiley & Sons, 2003). A psychology professor draws on theory and personal experience as a car salesman.

Resistance and Persuasion. By Eric S. Knowles and Jay A. Linn (Lawrence Erlbaum, 2004). Analyzes the nature of resistance and demonstrates how the knowledge of it can promote persuasion.

Selecting an Advertising Agency. By Stanley Beals and David Beals (Association of National Advertisers, Inc., 2002). A guide for clients that may also help agencies pitching them.

Sign Wars: The Cluttered Landscape of Advertising. By Robert Goldman and Stephen Papson (Guilford Press, 1995). Deconstructs the strategies used to distinguish one brand name from another by the use of commodity signs.

The Sponsor. By Eric Barnouw (Oxford University Press, 1978). Examines the power of the companies who fund television commercials.

Strategic Advertising Campaigns (2nd Ed). By Don E. Schultz, Dennis Martin, and William P. Brown (NTC Business Books, 1987). The fundamentals of formulating and implementing comprehensive campaigns.

The Tangled Web They Weave: Truth, Falsity, and Advertisers. By Ivan L. Preston (The University of Wisconsin Press, 1994). This critique states that false or misleading claims in advertisements can be perfectly legal.

Tested Advertising Methods (5th Ed.). By John Caples and Fred E. Hahn (Prentice-Hall, 1997). Latest edition of a classic on writing ads and proving their effectiveness.

Trends in Agency Compensation (12th Ed.). By David Beals and Robert H. Lundin (Association of National Advertisers, Inc., 2001). Triennial survey includes information on methods of compensation, the use of performance incentives, and the management of agency compensation.

Truth, Lies & Advertising: The Art of Account Planning. By Jon Steel (John Wiley & Sons, 1998). Argues for the importance of consumers' input into the making of ads.

Truth Well Told: McCann-Erickson and the Pioneering of Global Advertising. By Stewart Alter (McCann-Erickson Worldwide, 1995). The book's title has been the McCann-Erickson agency's motto since 1926.

20 Ads That Shook The World. By James B. Twitchell (Crown Publishers, 2000). Colorful, memorable ads from the 20th century.

Type & Layout: How Typography and Design Can Get Your Message Across-Or Get in the Way. By Colin Wheildon (Strathmoor Press, 1995). This layout primer uses ample illustrations to make its points.

Unconscious for Sale: Advertising, Psychoanalysis, and the Public. By Doris-Louise Haineault (University of Minnesota Press, 1993). Psychoanalytic interpretation of advertising as a successful model for the fundamental operations of the human psyche.

Visual Persuasion: The Role of Images in Advertising. By Paul Messaris (Sage Publications, 1997). Explores the visual aspects of marketing.

The Want Makers: Inside the World of Advertising. By Eric Clark (Penguin Books, 1988). A thorough, contentious study of modern advertising worldwide.

Whatever Happened to Madison Avenue? Advertising in the '90s. By Martin Mayer (Little, Brown and Company, 1991). Documents the decline of New York as the center of advertising.

When Ads Work: New Proof That Advertising Triggers Sales. By John Phillip Jones (Lexington Books, 1995). With a device called short-term advertising strength (STAS), measures the immediate effect of advertising on sales.

Where the Suckers Moon: An Advertising Story. By Randall Rothenberg (Alfred A. Knopf, 1994). Chronicles the brief relationship between Subaru and the agency hired to revive it.

Periodicals

AdAge Information on advertising from business and creative perspectives. (http://www.adage.com)

Adbusters Explores the culture of media and the effects it has on society and the environment. (http://www.adbusters.org)

Advertising and Marketing Review Source for information on marketing, economic and demographic data. (http://www.ad-mkt-review.com)

Adweek News and critiques on the week's ads. (http://www.adweek.com)

Boards Magazine   Focuses on the creative side of ad creation. (http://www.boardsmag.com)

Business Journals   Business news in midsized cities. (http://www.bizjournals.com)

CMYK   A magazine on visual design and communication. (http://www.cmykmag.com)

Communication Arts   Promotes the creative side of communication. (http://www.commarts.com)

DMNews   Explores the trends and technologies in marketing. (http://www.dmnews.com)

Editor and Publisher   Covers the newspaper industry. (http://www.editorandpublisher.com)

Great Cross Compiler   Covers the worlds of business and technology. (http://www.gccnews.com)

Guerilla Marketing   Offers new strategies in marketing. (http://www.gmarketing.com)

Incentive Magazine   Focused on business and employee management as well as marketing.   (http://www.incentivemag.com)

The Journal of Empirical Generalisations in Marketing   Reports on research related to the science of marketing and consumer behavior.   (http://www.empgens.com)

Media Inc.   Promotes multimedia advertising and creative work. (http://www.media-inc.com)

Media Life   Covers the media industry. (http://www.medialifemagazine.com)

Newsletter Access   Promotes communication and marketing via newsletters in all areas.   (http://www.newsletteraccess.com)

O'Dwyer's Public Relations News   Focuses mainly on public relations.   (http://www.odwyerpr.com)

Promo Manazine   Concentrates on both business and media marketing.   (http://www.promomagazine.com)

Response Magazine   Analysis and promotion of direct-response marketing.   (http://www.responsemagazine.com)

Target Marketing   Gives readers insights into all forms of marketing. (http://www.targetmarketingmag.com)

ZD Net   Focuses on media technology.   (http://www.zdnet.com)

Web Sites

Absolute Stock Photo   Photo source that offers a one-time-use option in addition to the standard royalty-free and rights-managed licensing.   (http://www.absolutestockphoto.com)

Ad*Access Images and database information for over 7,000 advertisements printed in U.S. and Canadian newspapers and magazines between 1911 and 1955. (http://www.library.duke.edu/digitalcollections/adaccess)

Adaholic Provides a searchable database of thousands of collectible magazine advertisements.available for purchase. (http://www.adaholic.com)

The Ad Feed A filter and showcase for standout advertising for all media. (http://www.theadfeed.com)

Adland With its tagline "all the adnews not fit to print," the site is a source for thousands of TV ads, current and historic. (http://www.adland.tv/index.php)

Adliterate Self-proclaimed "provocative" site providing radical thinking for the branding business. (http://www.adliterate.com)

Adpulp Online trade magazine covering all forms of marketing communication. (http://www.adpulp.com)

All Advertising Agencies Allows users to search quickly for agencies based on services, industry, budget, and zip code. (http://www.alladvertisingagencies.com)

Best on the Web Touting its strict standards for site, BOTW is a comprehensive directory categorizing content-rich, well designed Web sites. (http://www.botw.org)

Brand Flakes for Breakfast A blog of the ad agency Plain, BFFB provides offbeat news, ideas, design, branding, and industry gossip. (http://www.brandflakesforbreakfast.com)

Chaos Scenario A blog offering insight into the "chaos" resulting from the forces of technology, consumer apathy and marketing integration. (http://www.chaosscenario.com)

Coloribus Archive of over two million contemporary print, outdoor, television, and viral ads, plus a global winners showcase. (http://www.coloribus.com)

Design Firms A comprehensive directory of Web designers, graphic designers, and other professionals in design. (http://www.designfirms.org)

ihaveanidea With content generated exclusively by advertising pros, the site provides interviews, original articles, and community-building events. (http://www.ihaveanidea.org)

The Imaginary World A whimsical archive of images from vintage print ads, packaging, store displays, and more. (http://www.theimaginaryworld.com)

Osocio   A directory of social advertising and nonprofit campaigns from around the globe.   (http://www.osocio.org)

Random Culture   A resource for business and social news, advertising trends, and links to other good sources. (http://www.randomculture.com)

24-7 Press Release   A press-release distribution service that partners with PR Newswire for broad exposure. (http://www.24-7pressrelease.com)

Index